Studying God's Word

Book G

A Chronological Study

on the Message and Ministry

of the Lord Jesus Christ

Darrel A. Trulson

A publication of

Christian Liberty Press

502 West Euclid Avenue

Arlington Heights, Illinois 60004

Written by

Darrel A. Trulson

Scripture references are conformed to The Holy Bible, King James Version.

Printed in the United States of America

To my

Teacher
Friend
Guide and
Father

Thank you Dad for everything

Table of Contents

Table of Contents

Acknowledgments

When working on a project of this scope, there are inevitably many people to thank. As the <u>Studying God's Word</u> series grows and matures, I am continually brought to terms with my own inadaquacies, not only as a writer but as a person. Were it not for the love, support and encouragement of my friends and colleagues, these books would never be written. So to everyone who has not only stood behind me, but also been an integral and necessary part of this project, I give you my deepest and warmest heart-felt thanks.

Many thanks to Mike McHugh for his invaluable friendship, direction and guidance; Paul Lindstrom for his cooperation and understanding; Susan Grunwald, Carla Watschke, Cindy Watschke, Cheryl Justy and Dave Smith for their positive critique and comments during the editing, reviewing and rewriting of this book.

Thank you to Mark Dove for his cooperation when it came to sharing the Macintosh. Tell you what, next time you can use it from 12:00 a.m. to 4:00 a.m.

Thanks to Betty Dyson for her promotion of the S.G.W. series. If Pepsi had you for their sales manager they would be ahead of Coke by now.

A special thanks to the whole cast and crew of the CLASS Enrollment & Finance, and Shipping & Receiving Departments. Your patience and cooperation have been greatly appreciated. Thank you for doing your jobs so well so that my job is easier. Thank you for being the rack upon which I can hang my hats. More than ever, thank you for your support.

I especially want to thank Eric Pfeiffelman for his endless hours of dedication, design and development. The lines have never looked straighter and the text has never looked neater. Thank you for all your comments, creative insight, and suggestions. I also want to thank Deanna Davisson for her detailed editing and grammatical assistance. If there are any grammar mistakes or typos then they slipped by one of the best.

Finally I want to thank my wife Debbie, and my four boys, Derek, Daniel, Joshua and Michael for their love, patience and understanding. My love for you grows with each and every passing day. Thank you for being there by my side, helping me to maintain my perspective.

Preface

One of the primary goals of the *Studying God's Word* series is to encourage students to conform their thinking to the standard of God's revealed Word. When students begin to bring every one of their thoughts into captivity to God's Word, they begin to realize the joy of being conformed to the image of Jesus Christ.

In this series, a strong emphasis is placed on the need for young people to develop strong Christian character traits. Students are not only presented with important facts and truths from the Bible, they are also provided with a wealth of personal examples from the lives of God's people that illustrate the truths they need to comprehend.

In addition, this series utilizes a chronological approach to Bible study so young people can better understand the timing and order of the key events listed throughout the Bible. This approach permits students to gain an accurate understanding of the flow of events contained in the Bible.

It has often been said that these are the times that try men's souls. Modern American culture is confronting God's people, both young and old alike, with many challenging trials and temptations. More than ever before, young people need to be equipped with the whole armor of God's Word so they can withstand the fiery darts of the wicked one. May the Lord use this Bible Study series to equip his children with the spiritual weapons that they need to fight the good fight of faith.

Michael J. McHugh
Curriculum Director

Dr. Paul D. Lindstrom
Superintendent of Schools

How To Use This Book

If you are like most people, you may forget to read the instructions or directions for something until you are half finished with it and then discover you did something wrong. In order to understand this book and learn the most from it, **please read this section first!**

There are several types of learning tools woven into this book; each has a specific intention and purpose. The main body of the book consists of Bible lessons. These are taken from the Gospels of Matthew, Mark, Luke and John. Each lesson begins with either a map line or time line. The map line identifies specific locations pertinent to the lesson and gives general information concerning the events of the lesson. The time line lists the historical events surrounding the life of Christ. Both these tools are presented in an effort to tie together the events that take place within the Bible. A complete presentation of the time line is given in Appendix A.

Following the map line or time line, the lesson will contain the goal, memory verse, and background text. The student is to read the background text before continuing with the lesson. It is up to the individual teacher to decide if the verse is to be memorized for each lesson. All memory verses, lessons, and questions are written to be used with the King James Version of the Bible.

Each lesson will contain a few paragraphs in which the author suggests a few principles from the text and applications for the student. This is followed by several questions covering the background reading, thought questions, and lesson review questions. Some lessons will have supplemental exercises for the student to do.

Each of the four Gospels will have a background section that will explain the individual characteristics of the book. Although there are no questions in these sections, they need to be studied and understood to receive a complete understanding of God's Word. The lesson review will ask questions about the background sections.

There is a unit test after every fourteen lessons (a total of four unit tests throughout the book). Unit tests should be taken without the help of this book, the Bible, or any outside source. The questions in the unit test will be a combination of questions already asked in the lessons. Each unit test will only cover the subject matter presented in that unit.

Introduction to the Chronological Method of Bible Study

Welcome to one of the most important discoveries you will ever make, the discovery of God's Word. Throughout your life, you will have the opportunity to study the Bible. Each time you do, the Holy Spirit will be there to guide and direct your thoughts to help you to learn and grow in the Lord Jesus Christ. It is the hope and prayer of everyone involved in producing this book that through your study you will grow in the wisdom and understanding of God (Ephesians 1:17-19).

In order to make studying the Bible more interesting and profitable, this book is written to follow the Gospels in a Historical - Chronological pattern. We believe it is of utmost importance to you, the student, that as you study the Bible, you understand how all the separate stories and books fit together. Imagine a large jigsaw puzzle of a beautiful mountain village. If you were to take a few pieces from different points and study them individually, could you understand what the complete picture was? Of course not. You need to see all the pieces in the correct pattern in order to understand the "big picture." The Bible is the same way. If all we do is read one story here and another one there, we will not understand the true meaning of God's Word. We have to look at the Bible completely and study it as one unit in order to understand the "big picture."

Regrettably, time and space do not allow us to cover the complete New Testament in this book. The first part of the New Testament from Matthew to John is reviewed in this study. The rest of the New Testament, which covers the book of Acts and the Epistles, is reviewed in _Studying God's Word Book H_ and _Studying God's Word Book I._

The goal and purpose of this book comes directly from Joshua 1:8: "This book of the Law shall not depart out of thy mouth, but thou shalt meditate therein day and night, that thou mayest observe to do according to all that is written therein: for then thou shalt make thy way prosperous, and then thou shalt have good success." May the Lord grant you good success and wisdom as you study His Word through this book.

The Coming King
Lesson #1

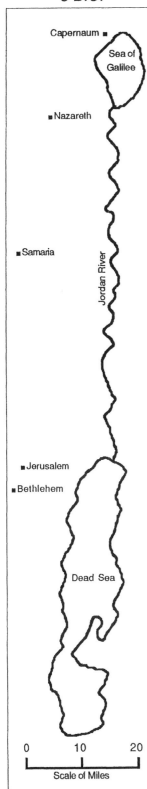

5 B.C.

Capernaum ■

Sea of Galilee

■ Nazareth

■ Samaria

Jordan River

■ Jerusalem

■ Bethlehem

Dead Sea

0   10   20

Scale of Miles

<u>Lesson Goal</u>: To understand that the Messiah was foretold as the hope for His people.

<u>Background Text</u>: John 1:1-14

<u>Memory Verse</u>: And the Word was made flesh, and dwelt among us, and we beheld His glory, the glory as of the only begotten of the Father, full of grace and truth. John 1:14

Approximately four hundred years had passed between the time when Malachi wrote to the nation of Israel, and when the angel announced to Mary that she would give birth to the Messiah. During this period the nation of Israel experienced a great deal of conflict and was eventually taken over and ruled by the Romans. This was a discouraging time for the Jewish people because many felt that they were either forgotten or abandoned by God. Their hope rested in the anticipation of the coming of the new King of Israel, God's Messiah.

Centuries before the birth of Christ in Bethlehem, a promise was given to the people: The Messiah would come to earth and save them from their sins. Psalms 130:7-8 says, "Let Israel hope in the Lord for with the Lord there is mercy, and with Him is plenteous redemption. And He shall redeem Israel from all his iniquities." This became a source of hope and encouragement for the people in the midst of hard times. They believed that no matter how difficult things became, God would some day send a deliverer to save them.

In order to understand the purpose of Christ's coming, a knowledge of the atonement and the Old Testament sacrificial system is necessary. During the Old Testament period, the Israelites would seek forgiveness for their sins on the Day of Atonement. On that day, the High Priest would enter the Holy of Holies, in the temple, and sprinkle animal blood over the Ark of the Covenant. This was to cover the sins of the people for that year. This was only a temporary remedy for the problem of sin. Since the sins were only forgiven for a short time, the people did not experience total redemption. Redemption is the complete deliverance from the consequences of sin. By sacrificing an animal and sprinkling its blood over the ark, temporary forgiveness was given; however, sacrifices were still necessary. The blood of animals was not sufficient to take away man's sins (Hebrews 10:4). It was only when Christ came as the ultimate sacrifice that man experienced complete and total forgiveness for his transgressions.

Although no one knew Who the Messiah would be, the prophecies, written hundreds of years earlier, told the people that the Messiah would be: out of the tribe of Judah (Genesis 49:10), from the family of Jesse (Isaiah 11:1), from the lineage of David (II Chronicles 7:18), born of a virgin (Isaiah 7:14), born in Bethlehem (Micah 5:2), and forced to flee to Egypt (Hosea 11:1; Matt. 2:15). Those who understood the teachings of Scripture knew that the prophecies would soon be fulfilled. This provided the nation of Israel with a sense of hope that it would soon be fully justified before the Lord.

Today as Christians, we have an eternal assurance that through the shed blood of Christ, our sins are completely forgiven. This forgiveness comes through the cross and our belief that Jesus Christ is God's Son and the Lord of our lives. Through Him we have salvation and the gift of everlasting life in heaven.

Questions: Multiple choice -- circle the correct answer for each question.

1. Who was the Word? (John 1:1)
    *John
    *Malachi
    *God
    *Israel

2. What did the Word create? (John 1:3)
    *Animals
    *All things
    *Plants
    *Birds

3. What was the Light of men? (John 1:4)
    *God
    *Death
    *John
    *Life

4. Into what does the Light shine? (John 1:5)
    *The hearts of men
    *The darkness
    *The heavens
    *The land of Israel

5. Who was the witness sent from God? (John 1:6-7)
    *Jesus
    *John
    *David
    *Isaiah

6. What was the job the true Light had? (John 1:9)
    *To overthrow the Roman empire
    *To raise the dead
    *To lighteth every man that cometh into the world
    *To tell parables

7. What did the world do when it saw the Word? (John 1:10)
    *Accepted Him
    *Nothing, because it did not recognize Him
    *Loved Him like a brother
    *Treated Him like a friend

8. What did He give those that would receive Him? (John 1:12)
    *He gave them power to become the sons of God.
    *He gave them glory and honor.
    *He gave them nothing.
    *He gave them long life.

9. Of what are the children of God born? (John 1:13)
    *Blood
    *God
    *Will of man
    *Will of the flesh

10. When the Word was made flesh, what did the people behold? (John 1:14)
    *Evil
    *His weakness
    *His glory
    *His love for children

Thought Questions:

1. Why do you feel it was necessary for Christ to come to the earth? _____

_____

_____

2. Do you feel that Christ's forgiveness allows you to do whatever you want? Explain your answer. _____

_____

_____

_____

Supplemental Exercise: Complete the crossword with the answers to the questions listed below.

1-D   Where did the light shine? (John 1:5)

2-A   There was a man _____ from God. (John 1:6)

3-A   What kind of light lighteth every man? (John 1:9)

4-D   To whom did He give power to become the sons of God? (John 1:12)

5-D   When was the Word? (John 1:1)

5-A   The same came for a witness to _____ witness of the light. (John 1:7)

6-A   The Word was with whom? (John 1:1)

7-D   He came unto his own, and his own _____ him not. (John 1:11)

8-D   For what did John come? (John 1:7)

8-A   Who were born, not of blood, nor of the _____ of the flesh. (John 1:13)

9-A   There was a man sent from God, whose _____ was John. (John 1:6)

10-D All things were _____ by Him. (John 1:3)

11-D What was in Him? (John 1:4)

12-D What did He do with His glory? (John 1:14)

12-A Who were _____, not of blood. (John 1:13)

13-A What did the Word do among us? (John 1:14)

14-D And the light shineth in darkness; and the darkness comprehended it _____. (John 1:5)

John's Birth Announced
Lesson #2

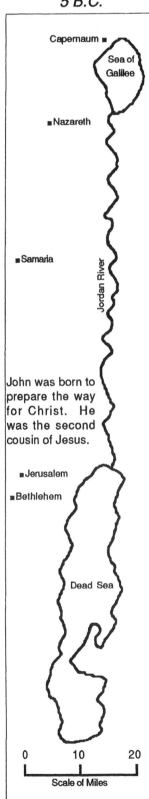

5 B.C.

Capernaum ■

Sea of Galilee

■Nazareth

■Samaria

Jordan River

John was born to prepare the way for Christ. He was the second cousin of Jesus.

■Jerusalem

■Bethlehem

Dead Sea

0   10   20

Scale of Miles

Lesson Goal: To understand that nothing is too difficult with God.

Background Text: Luke 1:5-25, 57-80

Memory Verse: For with God nothing shall be impossible. Luke 1:37

Has anything ever surprised or shocked you so much that you were left speechless? This literally happened to Zacharias when the angel told him that he and his wife, Elisabeth, were going to have a baby. Now there is nothing unusual about a woman becoming pregnant; however, Elisabeth was very old, and for her to give birth to a child would take a miracle.

When the angel explained to Zacharias that Elisabeth was pregnant, Zacharias did not believe him. One would think that the mere presence of an angel would convince Zacharias that a miracle was about to happen. Still, Zacharias doubted the angel's message and as a result, he was left without speech until John was born.

This child was going to be very special. He was to prepare the hearts of the people for the coming Messiah. The appearance of John the Baptist was prophesied in Isaiah 40:3, "The voice of him that crieth in the wilderness, prepare ye the way of the Lord, make straight in the desert a highway for our God."

This is a good lesson for us. We must not doubt the power and purpose of God. An angel may not appear to us as one did to Zacharias, but we do have the Bible to communicate God's message to us and the Holy Spirit to guide our lives in His purpose and will. We often limit the working of the Lord in our lives because we do not have enough faith to believe the things His Word tells us. It would be wise for us to learn from Zacharias' experience and not doubt the Bible, for nothing is too difficult with God.

<u>Questions</u>: Multiple choice -- circle the correct answer for each question.

1. What was the priest's duty when he went into the temple? (Luke 1:9)
      *Pray three times
      *Sacrifice a lamb
      *Tithe 1/10 of his possessions
      *Burn incense

2. Where was the angel when he appeared before Zacharias? (Luke 1:11)
      *In front of the alter
      *On the right side of the altar
      *On the left side of the altar
      *Behind the altar

3. What did the angel have to tell him? (Luke 1:13)
      *Zacharias shall become a High Priest.
      *Jesus shall soon be born.
      *There shall be a great earthquake.
      *Elisabeth shall have a son, and his name shall be called John.

4. What was the reaction of Zacharias at the time the angel told him the news? (Luke 1:18)
      *He questioned the angel.
      *He fainted.
      *He jumped for joy.
      *He was saddened.

5. What was the angel's name? (Luke 1:19)
      *Michael
      *Gabriel
      *Jonah
      *David

6. What was the punishment for Zacharias' unbelief? (Luke 1:20)
      *He was cut off from his family.
      *He was unable to speak until Elisabeth had her baby.
      *There was no punishment.
      *He was no longer a priest.

7. For how many months did Elisabeth hide herself? (Luke 1:24)
    *Three months
    *Five months
    *Six months
    *Five months

8. On what day did they circumcise the child? (Luke 1:59)
    *13th day
    *6th day
    *8th day
    *10th day

9. What did Zacharias call John? (Luke 1:76)
    *The son of Zacharias
    *The cousin of Jesus
    *John the Baptist
    *Prophet of the Highest

10. What was John to give God's people? (Luke 1:77)
    *Knowledge of salvation
    *Salvation
    *Forgiveness of sins
    *Freedom from the Roman Empire

Thought Questions:

1. In what areas of your life do you sometimes doubt God? _____

   _____

   _____

   _____

2. What are ways that you can strengthen your faith in the power of God? _____

   _____

   _____

   _____

   _____

Lesson Review:

1. On what day would the High Priest enter the Holy of Holies? (Lesson #1)_____

   _____

2. Give three references of prophecies foretelling Who the Messiah would be.

   (Lesson #1) _____

   _____

No Earthly Father
Lesson #3

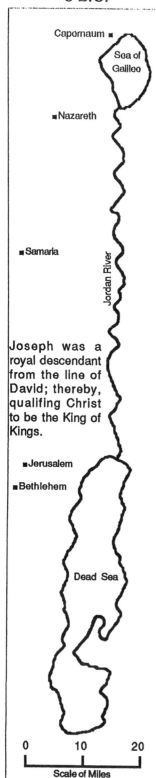

5 B.C.

Capernaum ■

Sea of Galilee

■ Nazareth

Jordan River

■ Samaria

Joseph was a royal descendant from the line of David; thereby, qualifing Christ to be the King of Kings.

■ Jerusalem

■ Bethlehem

Dead Sea

0   10   20

Scale of Miles

Lesson Goal: To understand the purpose for the virgin birth.

Background Text: Luke 1:26-56

Memory Verse: And, behold, thou shalt conceive in thy womb, and bring forth a Son, and shalt call His name Jesus. Luke 1:31

When the angel appeared to Mary announcing that she would conceive and give birth to God's Son, the prophecy foretold in Isaiah 7:14 was fulfilled, "Therefore the Lord Himself shall give you a sign; Behold, a virgin shall conceive, and bear a Son, and shall call His name Immanuel."

Why was it so necessary that the Messiah be born of a virgin? The answer to this goes all the way back to the first man. When Adam sinned, all mankind was condemned to death. Romans 5:12 says, "Wherefore, as by one man sin entered into the world, and death by sin; and so death passed upon all men, for that all have sinned." This sin nature, resulting in spiritual death, was passed down to all of Adam's descendants. You do not become a sinner when you reach a certain age, or when you commit your first sin. You were already a sinner before you were born.

When you were conceived, the sin nature that you inherited did not come from your mother, but from your father. It was not Eve's sin that condemned mankind to death; it was Adam's. Therefore, it was necessary that Christ be born of a virgin and have no earthly father, in order for Him to avoid inheriting the sin nature. Christ was conceived and born into the world holy and blameless, without any sin or blemish, so that He could eventually be the perfect sacrifice for our sins when He died on the cross.

There is nothing that we can do in our own selves to take the sin out of our lives. Many people think, "It is not my fault. Adam was the one who sinned, not me. Why should I be punished for his mistake?" We are punished for Adam's

sin because we are his descendants. For example, if both your parents have brown eyes, most likely when you were born, you inherited their brown eyes. You did not have any choice in the matter. You received the brown eyes because they were part of your family's gene make-up, and that was what you inherited. Sin works the same way. You get it whether or not you ask for it. It is part of the inherited curse that came down from Adam.

In the same way, we are given the free gift of redemption through Christ Jesus. There is nothing we have to do to earn it, no special tasks or responsibilities to perform. We simply need to believe upon Christ as our Savior and Lord. Without the virgin birth, none of this would have been possible. Thanks be to God that grace reigned in righteousness through Jesus Christ our Lord (Romans 5:21).

Questions:

1. In what month did the angel visit Mary? (Luke 1:26) _____

2. What did the angel say shall happen to Mary? (Luke 1:31) _____
   _____

3. Over what house shall He reign? (Luke 1:33) _____
   _____

4. How would Mary conceive? (Luke 1:35) _____
   _____

5. Where did Mary's journey take her? (Luke 1:39-40) _____
   _____

6. What happened to Elisabeth when she greeted Mary? (Luke 1:41) _____
   _____
   _____

7. What shall all generations call Mary? (Luke 1:48) _____
   _____

8. To whom is Jesus' mercy directed? (Luke 1:50) _____
   _____

9. What shall Jesus do to the mighty and to them of low degree? (Luke 1:52) ____
   _____
   _____

10. How long did Mary stay with Elisabeth? (Luke 1:56) _____

No Earthly Father

<u>Thought Questions</u>:

1. Do you feel it is important for you to take the responsibility for your mistakes? Explain your answer._____

_____

_____

_____

2. How can Christ cleanse you from your sins? _____

_____

_____

_____

_____

<u>Lesson Review</u>:

1. Why was it a miracle that Elisabeth was going to have a baby? (Lesson #2) ___

_____

2. Why is it necessary to understand the Old Testament sacrificial system? (Lesson #1) _____

_____

_____

<u>Supplemental Exercise</u>: Uncode the symbols to understand the message. The key is in Appendix B.

_____

_____

_____

_____

_____

Joseph's Righteous Action
Lesson #4

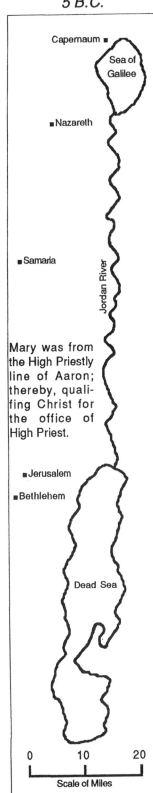

5 B.C.

Capernaum ■

Sea of Galilee

■ Nazareth

Jordan River

■ Samaria

Mary was from the High Priestly line of Aaron; thereby, quali-fing Christ for the office of High Priest.

■ Jerusalem

■ Bethlehem

Dead Sea

0   10   20

Scale of Miles

Lesson Goal: To understand that when God's Word speaks to us, we need to act upon it immediately.

Background Text: Matthew 1:18-25

Memory Verse: Behold, a virgin shall be with child, and shall bring forth a Son, and they shall call His name Emmanuel, which being interpreted is, God with us. Matthew 1:23

Imagine what Joseph must have felt when the angel appeared to him announcing that Mary was pregnant and would soon give birth to the Messiah. Initially he must have been concerned, perhaps confused, and maybe a little scared. In those days, if a woman became pregnant before being married, she could have been stoned to death.

Of course Joseph loved Mary, and did not want this to happen. However, what would everyone say about the fact that Mary was pregnant? Some people would not believe the fact that Mary's child was God's own beloved Son. They would think that she had sinned by having sex before she was married.

Joseph had a very difficult decision to make. Compare his response to that of Zacharias (Luke 1:18). Although Zacharias doubted the angel, Joseph believed his message and did all he could to take care of Mary. Matthew 1:24 says that Joseph arose from his sleep and did as the angel of the Lord commanded. He did not wait until morning or a later time to respond to the angel's message. He immediately acted upon the Word of the Lord.

What is our response to God's Word? When presented with teaching from Scripture, do we immediately do as it commands, or do we wait until we feel it is a better time? Let us say, for example, that after reading the Bible, the Holy Spirit leads you to witness to a neighborhood friend. Do you instinctively begin thinking of ways to go over and see your neighbor, or do you find excuses and reasons why you should not share the gospel with your friend?

Joseph's Righteous Actions

It is said that actions speak louder than words, and in the case of Joseph that was certainly true. His actions demonstrated a strong belief in the Word of God. There was no second guessing where Joseph was concerned. As soon as he received the Word of the Lord and understood it, he acted upon it.

Questions:

1. Joseph was the son of whom? (Matt. 1:16) _____

2. When was Mary found with child? (Matt. 1:18) _____
_____

3. What was Joseph going to do with Mary? (Matt. 1:19) _____
_____

4. What happened to Joseph when he thought on these things? (Matt. 1:20) ____
_____

5. What did the angel say to him concerning Mary? (Matt. 1:20) _____
_____
_____

6. What was Jesus called to do? (Matt. 1:21) _____

7. What was spoken of the Lord by the prophet? (Matt. 1:23) _____
_____
_____

8. What does Emmanuel mean? (Matt. 1:21) _____

9. What did Joseph do when he woke up? (Matt. 1:24) _____
_____

10. What did Joseph call Mary's firstborn son? (Matt. 1:25) _____

Thought Questions:

1. When God's Word tells you to do something, what is your response to it? _____
_____
_____
_____

2. When was the last time you told one of your friends or neighbors about the Lord Jesus? How did they respond? _____
_____
_____
_____
_____

Lesson Review:

1. Explain why your sin nature is inherited from your father and not your mother. (Lesson #3) _____

   _____

   _____

   _____

   _____

2. Why was it important that Jesus be born of a virgin? (Lesson #3) _____

   _____

   _____

   _____

   _____

3. Zacharias was of what genealogical line? (Lesson #2) _____

Supplemental Exercise: Find and circle the words listed in the word search puzzle. Words may be forward, backward, horizontal, vertical or diagonal.

```
H I R E B M A R I A C C D M L Q
P D V T Z B H J M R S O E T U B
E A S T V I R G I N I N V A A S
S W B A M R Y R A M V C E X L K
O J G N D T S A O I Y E I W Z S
J Q W G I H P E S O J I C S C O
Z K S E L S S T H S Y V N X D W
A N G L E X V S S Y O E O U W H
U I X E K S P O U O E D O K I S
T Y T U X O P E N E H P O S F K
Y S C N Z I S O W K S G S O E E
U T H A N B S U S E J S Y J G W
B V N M M C S N I S C X Q L X C
N V M M W I S K R O E A E I O O
M E A I J D E S U O P S E C B H
```

BIRTH	MARY	JOSEPH	ANGEL
CONCEIVED	ESPOUSED	WIFE	HOLY GHOST
JESUS	SAVE	VIRGIN	IMMANUEL
SON	SINS		

The Gift of Christmas
Lesson #5

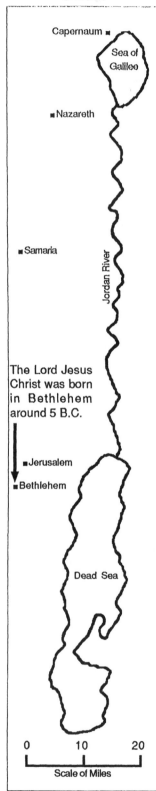

5 B.C.

Capernaum ■

Sea of Galilee

■Nazareth

■Samaria

Jordan River

The Lord Jesus Christ was born in Bethlehem around 5 B.C.

■Jerusalem

■Bethlehem

Dead Sea

0   10   20

Scale of Miles

Lesson Goal: To understand that the greatest gift we can give is ourselves every day of the year.

Background Text: Luke 2:1-20

Memory Verse: Glory to God in the highest, and on earth peace, good will toward men. Luke 2:14

To many of us, Christmas is the most enjoyable time of the year. We take the opportunity to give and receive gifts as a means of displaying our love and affection for other people. However, we should not limit the outward display of our appreciation to only this holiday. Every day we should open our hearts and give to people. Our thankfulness does not need to be limited to presents, we can give to others by our kind actions. Saying "Thank you," holding a door open for someone, or just helping our parents with dinner, are a few ways that we can give to others throughout the year.

Christmas is filled with such commercialism these days that we often lose sight of its true meaning. In reality, we give presents to other people because God gave us the greatest present of all. When Christ came to the earth, God was giving us that which meant the most to Him because He loved us so very much. When we give a present, it is generally some small toy or object that eventually breaks or wears out by the time the next Christmas arrives. I doubt if any of us has ever said, "Here, I give you my life as a present. Kill me if you want, but I am all yours." Even though this sounds kind of strange, this is what Christ meant when He said, "This is my body which is given for you." (Luke 22:19)

Christ, by coming to earth to die for our sins, was giving Himself as a sacrificial present to us. This sacrifice requires that we, in turn, give something back to God as a means of showing our appreciation for His gift. What is it then that God desires from us? Does He want us to give our time and offering to the church, to love our parents and family, to care for those who are sick and in need? Yes, God wants us to do these things, but this is not what God wants us to give to Him. The one thing that God requires back from us is our lives. Just as Christ gave His life for us, we are to give our lives back to God. Once we give our hearts to God, the good things that we do come as a natural expression of our love and gratitude for the Lord.

When we think of Christmas, let us not become so wrapped up in the festivities of gifts and presents that we neglect its true meaning. Let us take time out from the hectic schedule, go off to a room by ourselves, and thank God for His Gift by reaffirming our love to Him. This would be the greatest gift we could give God, not only on Christmas, but every day of the year.

Questions:

1. What did Caesar Augustus decree? (Luke 2:1) _____

    _____

2. When was this taxing first decreed? (Luke 2:2) _____

    _____

3. From what house and lineage was Joseph born? (Luke 2:4) _____

    _____

4. Why were the shepherds afraid? (Luke 2:9) _____

    _____

    _____

5. What did the angel say the sign would be? (Luke 2:12) _____

    _____

6. What did the heavenly host say when they praised God? (Luke 2:14) _____
   _____

7. Where did the shepherds find the babe? (Luke 2:15-16) _____
   _____

8. What was the reaction of those who heard the saying that was told to them by
   the angels? (Luke 2:18) _____
   _____

9. What was Mary's reaction to everything that had happened? (Luke 2:19) _____
   _____

10. Why were the shepherds glorifying and praising God? (Luke 2:20) _____
    _____

Thought Questions:

1. What can you do to demonstrate the true meaning of Christmas? _____
   _____
   _____
   _____
   _____

2. What is the greatest gift that you can give God? _____
   _____
   _____
   _____
   _____

Lesson Review:

1. How did Joseph feel when the angel appeared to him? (Lesson #4) _____
   _____

2. Did Zacharias' response to the angel's message please God? Why? (Lesson #2)
   _____
   _____
   _____
   _____

3. Explain how Psalms 130:7-8 offered Israel a source of hope. (Lesson #1) _____
   _____
   _____

<u>Supplemental Exercise</u>: Solve the logic problem.

Introduction to logic problems: The information you need to solve a logic problem is given in the introduction to each exercise and in the clues. Solving logic problems teaches you to take the given facts and through a process of reasoning and elimination discover the answers.

To start solving, read the introduction and the clues carefully. Next, enter into the solving chart all the information that you are given. Use an "X" to indicate a definite "no" and a "•" to indicate a definite "yes".

Some facts will be entered in more than one place in the chart. Filling in the chart will help you to narrow down the number of possible answers and may also reveal some new facts. Read the clues again and look for new relationships.

To continue solving, it may be necessary for you to make an assumption of fact. But because it is an assumption, you must look for contradictions, which mean that the assumption is false and you have eliminated one possibility.

Continue to search for new facts until you have solved the problem. Once you have started solving them, you will enjoy logic problems. The problems will become gradually more difficult as you continue through this book. If you are able to solve all the problems in this book, consider yourself a master at logic problems.

Logic Problem

On one sunny afternoon in Galilee, five happy couples got married. After the ceremonies, friends and families of the newlyweds celebrated in their respective villages. From the information given, can you determine the names of the bride and groom at each wedding and the village where the celebration took place?

1. Neither the newlywed couple of Judas and Lydia nor the one of Mary and her groom was married in Bethsaida.

2. Miriam, who did not marry Joseph, had a spectacular wedding in Nazareth.

3. Mark slept late and arrived breathlessly in Capernaum in the nick of time. His nervous bride was not Ruth or Mary.

4. Saul was married in Tiberias.

	Mark	Saul	Simon	Joseph	Judas	Cana	Nazareth	Capernaum	Bethsaida	Tiberias
Mary										
Martha										
Miriam										
Ruth										
Lydia										
Cana										
Nazareth										
Capernaum										
Bethsaida										
Tiberias										

Simeon's Dedication
Lesson #6

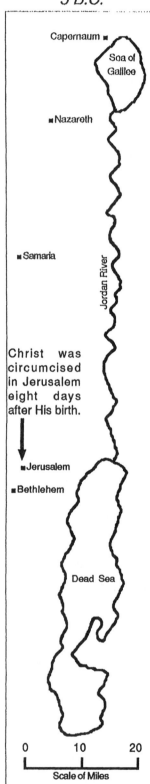

5 B.C.

Capernaum ■

Soa of Galilee

■ Nazareth

■ Samaria

Jordan River

Christ was circumcised in Jerusalem eight days after His birth.

■ Jerusalem

■ Bethlehem

Dead Sea

0   10   20

Scale of Miles

Lesson Goal: To understand that when we serve the Lord and commit our hearts to His will, our dreams will conform to God's desires.

Background Text: Luke 2:21-38

Memory Verse: Delight thyself also in the Lord, and He shall give thee the desires of thine heart. Psalms 37:4

When Simeon held the Christ child in his arms for the first time, he realized the fulfillment of a dream that he had believed for many years. His dream was to see the Messiah before he died. Simeon was an old man, but he understood the Old Testament prophecies which predicted the coming of the Messiah. When he saw Jesus in the temple, the Holy Spirit revealed to him that this was God's Son. What a wonderful experience this must have been! Simeon had seen the Messiah, and now he could pass on to eternity knowing that his dream had been fulfilled.

Many of us may have dreams and ambitions that we hold close to our hearts. Some may be silly, but others may be very important. As a child, I always wanted to be a baseball player. This never happened, but I still enjoy watching the sport. My sisters would play with their dolls and dream that they were beautiful young maidens, waiting for their Prince Charming to come and sweep them off their feet. Young children live in the world of "make believe" where anything can happen and where one's dreams become reality.

As we become adults, an unfortunate thing happens: dreams become lost in the midst of the daily work grind. Circumstances often do not permit the luxury of dreams because the hard facts of life and reality hit with a vengeance. James Thurber, in his acclaimed story, The Secret Life of Walter Mitty, displays a quiet, timid man who escapes the pressure of life by fantasizing that he is the Great American Hero. One time he dreams that he is a dangerous spy, and another time he thinks of himself as a famous navy boat captain. Mitty's dreams take him away from reality in order to help him cope with the pressures of life. Dreams and ambitions can be a good thing as long as we do not become like Walter Mitty, and mistake them for reality.

It is important to note that our dreams and desires may either lead us toward God or away from God. We should never place a greater emphasis upon them than we do upon the Lord Jesus Christ. It should be our desire to serve the Lord and love Him more every day. As we do this, our ambitions will conform to the desires God wants us to have (II Corinthians 3:18). As our memory verse says, when we do the things that please the Lord, He will give us the desires of our heart. God can do this because when we please Him, our dreams conform to His desires. So, God gives to us the good things which He would want us to have in the first place. In the case of Simeon, God fulfilled his dream because it was the Lord's desire.

Questions: Please indicate your answer with either True or False.

1. _____ After twelve days were accomplished for the circumcising of the Child, His name was called Jesus. (Luke 2:21)

2. _____ Every female that openeth the womb shall be called holy to the Lord. (Luke 2:23)

3. _____ It was revealed to Simeon that he shall not die till he sees the Christ. (Luke 2:26)

4. _____ Simeon came by the Spirit to Mary and Joseph's house to see the Christ. (Luke 2:27)

5. _____ Simeon proclaimed that Jesus is to be a light to the Gentiles. (Luke 2:32)

6. _____ Simeon blessed them and spoke unto Mary concerning Jesus. (Luke 2:34)

7. _____ Anna was a prophetess of young age at the time Jesus was born. (Luke 2:36)

8. _____ Anna was a widow of about fourscore and four years. (Luke 2:37)

9. _____ Anna served God in the temple where she prayed and fasted night and day. (Luke 2:37)

10. _____ Anna spoke about the Lord to those that looked for the redemption in Jerusalem. (Luke 2:38)

Thought Questions:

1. Do you have any dreams or desires? What are they? _____

_____

_____

_____

_____

2. How can you know whether God desires for you to have the dreams that you just listed? _____

_____

_____

_____

_____

Lesson Review:

1. Explain how Christ's coming to the earth and dying on the cross was a gift to His children. (Lesson #5) _____

_____

_____

_____

_____

2. How was Joseph's response to the angel's message different from that of Zacharias? (Lesson #4) _____

_____

_____

_____

3. Where was John until he showed himself to Israel? (Lesson #2) _____

_____

_____

Wise Men from the East
Lesson #7

3 B.C.

Capernaum ■

Sea of Galilee

■ Nazareth

■ Samaria

Jordan River

The Magi stopped first in Jerusalem to speak with Herod, then continued on to Bethlehem.

■ Jerusalem

■ Bethlehem

Dead Sea

0   10   20

Scale of Miles

Lesson Goal: To understand the purpose and the significance of the Magi.

Background Text: Matthew 2:1-12

Memory Verse: I have been young, and now am old; yet have I not seen the righteous forsaken, nor his seed begging bread. Psalms 37:25

Unlike the way most nativity scenes depict Christ's birth, the wise men did not visit Jesus the night He was born. The Magi actually came to Christ about two years after His birth. This would account for the fact that King Herod attempted to have all the male children, two years old and under, killed.

We do not know exactly how many Magi came to visit Christ. We tend to think that there were three wise men. At least that is what one of our Christmas carols says, "We three Kings of Orient are, bearing gifts we traverse afar..." There could have been several Magi that came to see Christ, including a caravan of servants and supplies necessary to make the long trip from the East.

The Magi were of great help to Joseph and Mary. Not only did their visit confirm to them that Christ was to be the King of Kings, but their presents of gold, frankincense and myrrh were financially valuable. The Lord, in His providence, took care of Mary and Joseph's needs by sending the Magi.

When we think of Christ, we see Him as our Savior and Lord. We forget that He was a child Who, though sinless, had needs that had to be met. Just as God graciously provided for the Christ child

Wise Men from the East

and His earthly parents, He also provides for us. Our circumstances may vary, but whatever our needs are, the Lord will take care of His righteous people. He does not forget or neglect His children. "But the Lord is faithful, who shall stablish you, and keep you from evil." (II Thessalonians 3:3)

This does not mean that we will not suffer or go through trials. Fleeing to Egypt for their lives was a trial for Joseph and his family. Traveling to Bethlehem and being forced to lay Jesus in a manger were trials for Mary. Dealing with Mary's pregnancy was a trial for Joseph. Still, in the midst of those difficulties, God was there and was faithful to His followers, establishing them and keeping them from evil and harm.

Questions: Match the correct answer with the proper question.

1. _____ Where was Jesus born? (Matt. 2:1)

2. _____ What did the wisemen see? (Matt. 2:2)

3. _____ How did Herod act when he heard the news? (Matt. 2:3)

4. _____ Who did King Herod gather together? (Matt. 2:4)

5. _____ Who did the priests and scribes quote? (Matt. 2:5)

6. _____ What did King Herod tell the wisemen to do? (Matt. 2:8)

7. _____ Where did the star take the wisemen? (Matt. 2:11)

8. _____ How did the wisemen act when they saw Jesus? (Matt. 2:11)

9. _____ What did the wisemen bring with them? (Matt. 2:11)

10. _____ How did God warn the wisemen? (Matt. 2:12)

a. Scribes and chief priests

b. House of Mary and Joseph

c. Troubled

d. Fell down and worshiped

e. Bethlehem of Judea

f. Search for the child and bring back word

g. Gold, Myrrh & Frankincense

h. A prophet

i. Star in the east

j. In a dream

<u>Thought Questions</u>:

1. What has God provided for you? _____

   _____

   _____

   _____

   _____

2. Do you think you should praise God for trials and difficult times? Explain your answer. _____

   _____

   _____

   _____

   _____

<u>Lesson Review</u>:

1. What was Simeon's dream? (Lesson #6) _____

   _____

2. What were the good tidings the angel brought to the shepherds? (Lesson #5) _

   _____

3. How did Mary conceive? (Lesson #3) _____

   _____

<u>Supplemental Exercise:</u> Uncode the symbols to understand the message. The key is in Appendix B.

_____

_____

_____

Christ in the Temple
Lesson #8

8 A.D.

Capernaum ■

Sea of Galilee

■ Nazareth

■ Samaria

Jordan River

While living in Nazareth at the age of twelve, Christ traveled to the temple in Jerusalem for Passover.

■ Jerusalem

■ Bethlehem

Dead Sea

0   10   20

Scale of Miles

Lesson Goal: To understand that Christ grew and matured in the same way as we do.

Background Text: Luke 2:41-52

Memory Verse: And Jesus increased in wisdom and stature, and in favour with God and man. Luke 2:52

As we study this passage regarding Christ's visit to the temple, we recognize that even at the early age of twelve, our Lord gave an indication of His future office. The people in the temple marveled at His wisdom. Christ had a knowledge of the Scriptures that surpassed even that of the priests and scribes. Is this to say then that since Christ was God, He had an immediate understanding of everything because of His omniscience? Luke 2:40 says that "The child grew, and waxed strong in spirit." This progress or advancement pertained to His human nature, for His divine nature could receive no increase. Our Lord subjected His soul and mind to ignorance so that He could be like us in every way (Hebrews 2:17).

Ignorance is not a curse of the sin nature. Adam, while in the perfect state, did not possess complete knowledge; nor do angels have unlimited understanding in the ways of God. There is a growth and maturing process that takes place in all of God's creatures. This maturing process was also evident in Christ Jesus. As a child, He had to study, memorize, learn and grow, just as we do every day of our lives.

The fact that Christ chose to remain ignorant did not mean that He was any less God. He did not sacrifice His deity for the sake of His humanity. Philippians 2:6-8 explains that Christ, as the second person of the Trinity, emptied Himself of His glory and willfully chose not to use parts of His divinity. In other words, Christ possessed complete deity but decided not to utilize it to its fullest. John Calvin has written in his commentary on the book of Luke, "If it takes nothing from his glory, that he was altogether 'emptied,'... neither does it degrade him, that he chose not only to grow

in body, but to make progress in mind. There is only this difference between us and him, that the weaknesses which press upon us, by a necessity which we cannot avoid, were undertaken by him voluntarily, and of his own accord."

So how was it then that Christ could possess such a knowledge of Scripture that it caused the people of the temple to marvel? Our Lord's understanding was made evident because He was fully committed to His heavenly Father's work. Christ was perfect in every way, and in His perfection He studied and grew to understand the teachings of Scripture. Our Lord made Himself an example for us to follow through His service to the heavenly Father. By our own study and understanding of the Bible, we will also grow in the wisdom and service of our Lord.

Questions:

1. Why did Christ's parents go to Jerusalem? (Luke 2:41) _____

   _____

2. At what age did Jesus go to Jerusalem? (Luke 2:42) _____

3. How far did Joseph and Mary go before they found that Jesus was not with them? (Luke 2:44) _____

   _____

4. After three days, where did they find Jesus? (Luke 2:46) _____

   _____

5. What was Jesus doing? (Luke 2:46) _____

   _____

6. How did Mary react to this? (Luke 2:48) _____

   _____

   _____

7. What was the response of Jesus? (Luke 2:49) _____

   _____

8. Did Joseph and Mary understand what Jesus said? (Luke 2:50) _____

9. Where did Jesus and His family go from there? (Luke 2:51) _____

10. In what did Jesus increase? (Luke 2:52) _____

Christ in the Temple

Thought Questions:

1. Why should you study the Bible? _____

_____

_____

_____

2. How can you grow and mature to be more like Christ? _____

_____

_____

_____

_____

Lesson Review:

1. What reason(s) could you give to support that the Magi came two years after Jesus was born? (Lesson #7) _____

_____

_____

2. How did the angel appear to Joseph? (Lesson #4) _____

3. Describe what happened on the Day of Atonement. (Lesson #1) _____

_____

_____

Supplemental Exercise: Complete the puzzle and find the hidden phrase.

And when He was [1] years old, they went up to Jerusalem after the [2] of the feast. And when they had fulfilled the days, as they returned, the child, Jesus, tarried behind in Jerusalem; and [3] and His [4] knew not of it. But they, supposing Him to have been in the company, went a day's journey; and they sought him among their [5] and acquaintance... And it came to pass that, after [6] [7], they found him in the temple, sitting in the midst of the doctors, both hearing them and asking them questions. (Luke 2:42-44, 46)

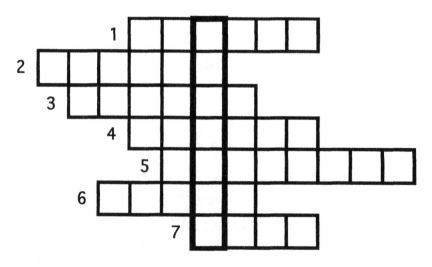

The Baptism of Christ
Lesson #9

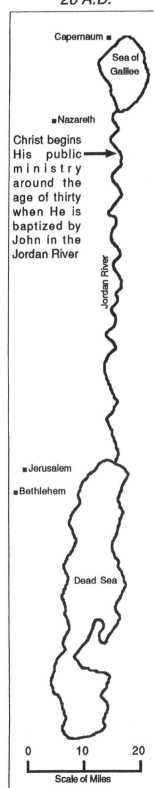

26 A.D.

Capernaum ■

Sea of Galilee

■ Nazareth

Christ begins His public ministry around the age of thirty when He is baptized by John in the Jordan River →

Jordan River

■ Jerusalem

■ Bethlehem

Dead Sea

0   10   20

Scale of Miles

Lesson Goal: To understand the nature of Christ and His baptism.

Background Text: Matthew 3:13-17; Mark 1:9-11; Luke 3:21-23

Memory Verse: And the Holy Ghost descended in a bodily shape like a dove upon Him, and a voice came from heaven, which said, Thou art my beloved Son; in Thee I am well pleased. Luke 3:22

It had been about eighteen years since Christ was found teaching in the temple. The New Testament is silent about our Lord during this time of His life. It is likely, however, that He helped Joseph, his earthly father, as a carpenter in the city of Nazareth; continued His study in the law and the prophets; and maintained the ritual of going to Jerusalem each year to celebrate the Passover.

Now the time had come for Christ to begin his earthly ministry. This started when John baptized Him in the Jordan River. God used baptism as an outward demonstration for the people to indicate that they had repented of their sins and turned to following God. This is why John was reluctant to baptize Jesus. He knew Christ had no sin of which to repent. Still, Christ sought the baptism as a sign that his ministry had begun.

The Baptism of Christ

Much discussion has centered on baptism and the role that this sacrament should play in the church. Should a person be immersed beneath the water, or is sprinkling on the head sufficient? Do we baptize infants or only adults? Volumes of books have been written on this topic so you can make this a personal study for yourself.

The issue that we must address is that baptism does not bring about salvation in a person's life. Baptism is an outward demonstration that a person is a covenantal member of God's family. Baptism cannot lead to salvation because then salvation would be on the basis of works. Once a person is baptized, the church is to help him in his spiritual walk so that he follows God.

In this passage we also have an excellent illustration of the doctrine of the Trinity. This is the doctrine that teaches that the divine nature consists of one God in three persons. Jesus Christ, the Son of God, was baptized; the Holy Spirit, as a dove, descended upon Christ; God the Father spoke and said, "This is my beloved Son." Each member of the Godhead had an active role in the baptism of Christ. Albert Barnes, in his commentary on the New Testament says, "It is impossible to explain these transactions consistently in any other way than by supposing that these are three equal persons in the divine nature or essence, and that each of these sustains an important part in the work of redeeming man."

There are many things in the Bible that are difficult to understand. The baptism of believers, the doctrine of the Trinity, the sovereignty of God, and the mystery of the gospel are just a few. These and many more doctrines like them sometimes take years of study to comprehend. The important thing to realize is that we do not have to understand everything about the Bible immediately, but that we must be willing to study and learn. The understanding will eventually come, whether here or in heaven.

Questions: Multiple choice -- circle the correct answer for each question.

1. Where was Jesus baptized? (Matt. 3:13)
    *Sea of Galilee
    *Euphrates River
    *Jordan River
    *Nile River

2. Who baptized Jesus? (Matt. 3:14-16)
    *John
    *Matthew
    *Luke
    *Herod

3. What descended upon Jesus? (Matt. 3:16)
    *A raven
    *A dove
    *A penguin
    *A pigeon

4. Where did Jesus come from before He was baptized? (Mark 1:9)
   *Nazareth of Galilee
   *Egypt
   *Assyria
   *The desert

5. What did the voice from heaven say at Jesus' baptism? (Mark 1:11)
   *Thou art my beloved Son, in whom I am well pleased.
   *This is the greatest Prophet in all of Israel.
   *This is the Deliverer for whom you have been waiting.
   *This is the next Roman Emperor.

6. Who spoke from heaven? (Mark 1:11)
   *A voice (God the Father)
   *Moses
   *Elijah
   *Michael

7. What opened up when Jesus was baptized? (Luke 3:21)
   *The earth
   *The heaven
   *The clouds
   *The ocean

8. Who descended upon Jesus? (Luke 3:22)
   *Moses
   *John the baptist
   *The Holy Ghost
   *Elias

9. About how old was Jesus at this time? (Luke 3:23)
   *20 years
   *30 years
   *35 years
   *40 years

10. Who was Joseph's father? (Luke 3:23)
    *Juda
    *Herodias
    *Philip
    *Heli

Thought Questions:

1. What does baptism mean to you? _____

_____

_____

2. Do you feel that it is important for you to understand everything in the Bible? Explain your answer. _____

_____

_____

_____

_____

_____

Lesson Review:

1. How many wisemen came to see Jesus? (Lesson #7) _____

_____

2. Where did Anna serve God? (Lesson #6) _____

3. Why did Jesus stay at the temple and astound the teachers? (Lesson #8) ____

_____

_____

Supplemental Exercise: Unscramble the six words listed below. Take the letters that are circled and rearrange them to solve the missing phrase. Clue: the missing phrase is from this lesson's story.

⬛⬛⬛⬛⬛⬛ IELLEGA

⬛⬛⬛⬛⬛⬛⬛ OVEBELED

⬛⬛⬛⬛⬛⬛ SLPEEAD

⬛⬛⬛⬛⬛⬛⬛ FEDURSEF

⬛⬛⬛⬛⬛⬛⬛⬛⬛⬛⬛ TSREOGUHSINES

⬛⬛⬛⬛ EOCIV

— — — — — — — — — — — — — — — — — —

The Temptation of Christ
Lesson #10

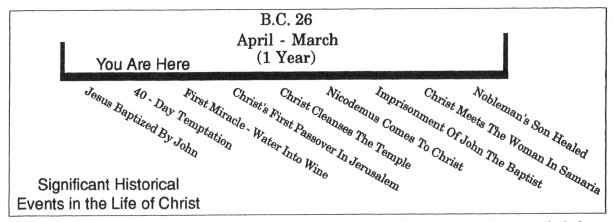

B.C. 26
April - March
(1 Year)

You Are Here

Jesus Baptized By John
40 - Day Temptation
First Miracle - Water Into Wine
Christ's First Passover In Jerusalem
Christ Cleanses The Temple
Nicodemus Comes To Christ
Imprisonment Of John The Baptist
Christ Meets The Woman In Samaria
Nobleman's Son Healed

Significant Historical
Events in the Life of Christ

Lesson Goal: To understand how we can stand against temptation and defeat Satan.

Background Text: Matthew 4:1-11; Mark 1:12-13; Luke 4:1-13

Memory Verse: Thy Word have I hid in mine heart, that I might not sin against thee. Psalms 119:11

The Bible records many temptations but there are two examples that stand out above all others. The first sin, when Satan tempted Adam and Eve in the garden of Eden, and the temptation of Christ in the wilderness.

Romans 5 and I Corinthians 15:45-47 describe Christ as the second Adam. Adam sinned and mankind was condemned to die; whereas, Christ purchased the means of redemption by not sinning when tempted, and by dying on the cross as the perfect sacrifice. It is necessary to understand the temptation of Christ within the context of Adam's sin. Christ, by not sinning, became the new Adam. No longer was man condemned by sin, but he now had salvation through the permanent atonement of Christ Jesus.

Through this illustration we have a practical model to follow when responding to temptation. First of all, we see that temptation is often the strongest soon after a spiritual victory. Forty days before His temptation was completed, Christ had been baptized by John, and proclaimed by God to be His beloved Son. Satan took advantage of Christ by tempting Him when He was physically weak and hungry in the wilderness.

I Corinthians 10:12 advises: "Let him that thinketh he standeth take heed lest he fall." If we consider ourselves to be great and become overconfident, then we will not be as attentive as we should, so as to resist temptation. If a commander of an army considered himself to be greater than his enemy, he may not take the necessary precautions to protect his men. The enemy, no matter how small, could take advantage of this and deliver a mortal wound. So then, we need to be careful not to become overconfident, but rather to be prepared to resist temptation.

Secondly, Satan will often tempt us by twisting the truth. One of the craftiest temptations that Satan can use against us is to present half-truths. He tries to convince us that sin is not really a sin, but a means to help ourselves. Consider how he tempted Christ to change the rocks to bread. This was a half-truth. There was nothing wrong with eating bread and performing miracles; however, Christ knew that it would be sinful to do it upon Satan's request, for selfish reasons.

We may be tempted to do something which is not sinful by itself, but could be wrong within the context of the temptation. For example, it may not be a sin to eat an apple or an orange. In fact, they are very good for us because they provide vitamins and nourishment. However, we may be tempted to eat an orange before supper, when we know that our mother would disapprove. The eating of the fruit has become a sin upon the disobedience to our parents' instruction.

Satan also twisted the truth by incorrectly interpreting the meaning of Scripture. When he quoted to Christ the passage from Psalms 91:11 - 12, he twisted its meaning to say something it was never intended to say. Satan will tempt us in the same fashion, by causing us to interpret Scripture in a different way than God intended. The incorrect interpretation of God's Word will not only make us confused concerning the meaning of Scripture, but it could easily lead us into sin.

Finally, notice how Christ responded to Satan and the temptation. He quoted the Scriptures. This is so important for us to consider. Satan despises the Word of God. Ephesians 6:17 describes the Word of God as a sword. With it we can thrust and jab to defend ourselves, and inevitably defeat Satan. A soldier, going to battle, will do all he can to sharpen his sword and improve his armor. In the same way, the more Scripture we have studied and memorized, the better weapon we will have against Satan.

Within the context of this passage, God has not only given us insight into the thoughts and feelings of His own Son, but He has also shown us a means to understand and resist temptation. Let us use what we have studied here and apply it to our lives every day.

Questions: Multiple choice -- circle the correct answer for each question.

1. Where did the Spirit lead Christ? (Matt. 4:1)
   *The wilderness
   *The desert
   *The mountains
   *The ocean

2. How long had Jesus fasted? (Matt. 4:2)
   *Thirty days and thirty nights
   *Twelve hours
   *Forty days and forty nights
   *Twenty days and twenty nights

3. Into what did the devil ask Jesus to turn the stones? (Matt. 4:3)
   *Meat
   *Bread
   *Berries
   *Water

4. At the second temptation, what did Satan want Jesus to do? (Matt. 4:6)
   *Fall down and worship Satan.
   *Acknowledge that Satan was God.
   *Turn stones into bread.
   *Cast Himself down.

5. What else besides Satan was with Jesus in the wilderness? (Mark 1:13)
   *Birds
   *Wild beasts
   *Lambs
   *Lots and lots of sand

6. How did Jesus feel after He fasted forty days? (Luke 4:2)
   *He felt fine
   *He hungered
   *He was tired
   *He was thirsty

7. If man does not live by bread alone, by what does man live? (Luke 4:4)
   *He lives by himself.
   *He lives by going to church on a regular basis.
   *He lives by obedience to his parents.
   *He lives by every word of God.

The Temptation of Christ

8. What did Satan show Jesus when they were on the mountain? (Luke 4:5)
    *The heavens
    *The kingdom of Jerusalem
    *The land of Israel
    *All the kingdoms of the world

9. What did the devil say he would give Jesus? (Luke 4:6)
    *Power and glory
    *Eternal life
    *Freedom to rule the Israelites
    *All the riches of the world

10. Who did Satan say would keep charge over Jesus? (Luke 4:10)
    *God
    *The angels
    *Joseph
    *The Holy Ghost

Thought Questions:

1. What do you do when you face temptation? _____

_____

_____

_____

_____

_____

_____

2. How do you use the Word of God as a sword? _____

_____

_____

_____

_____

_____

_____

Lesson Review:

1. When did Jesus begin His earthly ministry? (Lesson #9) _____

_____

2. Who was the man that held Christ in his arms? (Lesson #6) _____

3. Who decreed that all the world should be taxed? (Lesson #5) _____

_____

A Miracle of Quality
Lesson #11

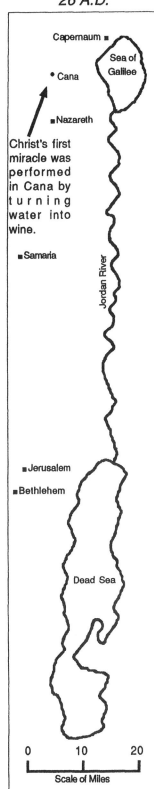

26 A.D.

Capernaum ■

Sea of Galilee

• Cana

■ Nazareth

Christ's first miracle was performed in Cana by turning water into wine.

■ Samaria

Jordan River

■ Jerusalem

■ Bethlehem

Dead Sea

0   10   20

Scale of Miles

Lesson Goal: To understand that Christ has the power to change things for the better.

Background Text: John 2:1-12

Memory Verse: Therefore if any man be in Christ, he is a new creature; old things are passed away; behold, all things are become new. II Corinthians 5:17

Let us use this first miracle performed by our Lord as means of introduction to the Gospel of John. John wrote as a lawyer trying to persuade his readers that Christ was the Messiah. Part of John's argument was to set forth seven miracles that the Lord performed to prove that He was God's Son. The first of these miracles was turning the water into wine at the wedding in Cana.

This was a miracle of quality. Christ demonstrated that He could transform an already existing element by changing it into something different or if necessary something better. He took water and instantaneously turned it into wine which was of the highest quality (John 2:10). The disciples, who were in attendance with Him at the wedding, saw this miracle. They were able to draw the conclusion that a superior being, Who had given proof to His claims by His acts of mercy and power, was among them.

Spiritually speaking, our Lord does the same thing when a person becomes a Christian. Christ takes a man dead in his trespasses and sins and transforms that person into a new creature. The prophet Ezekiel explains it best when he says, "And I will give them one heart, and I will put a new spirit within you; and I will take the stony heart out of their flesh, and will give them a heart of flesh" (Ezekiel 11:19). When we become Christians, our hearts are transformed. Whereas, before we had a heart that was dead in its sin, we now have a heart that is alive to God through Christ Jesus (Romans 6:11). Just as the water had no power to change itself into wine, so a man cannot purify his life by his own good works. It takes a miracle from our Lord to change the heart of a man.

A Miracle of Quality

<u>Questions:</u>

1. What took place in Cana of Galilee? (John 2:1) _____

2. Who was called to this occasion? (John 2:2) _____

3. What did the mother of Jesus say the people wanted? (John 2:3) _____

4. What did Jesus say had not yet come? (John 2:4) _____

5. Who were to do whatever Jesus asked? (John 2:5) _____

6. How many waterpots of stone were used? (John 2:6) _____

7. With what did Jesus say the waterpots were to be filled? (John 2:7) _____
_____

8. To whom did Jesus say to give the waterpots? (John 2:8) _____

9. What did the disciples do when they saw the miracle? (John 2:11) _____
_____

10. Who went down to Capernaum with Jesus? (John 2:12) _____

<u>Thought Questions:</u>

1. What changes can a person expect upon becoming a new person in Christ
Jesus? _____
_____
_____
_____
_____

2. Why is it that a man cannot purify his life by his own good works? _____
_____
_____
_____
_____

<u>Lesson Review:</u>

1. Describe how Christ is the second Adam. (Lesson #10) _____
_____
_____

2. At what age did Jesus teach in the temple? (Lesson #8) _____

3. What does the atonement mean? (Lesson #1) _____
_____
_____

Born Again
Lesson #12

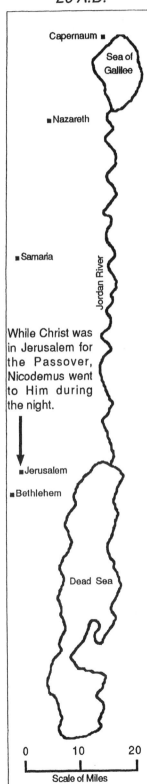

26 A.D.

Capernaum ■

Sea of Galilee

■ Nazareth

Jordan River

■ Samaria

While Christ was in Jerusalem for the Passover, Nicodemus went to Him during the night.

■ Jerusalem

■ Bethlehem

Dead Sea

0   10   20

Scale of Miles

Lesson Goal: To understand what it means to be born again.

Background Text: John 3:1-21

Memory Verse: For God so loved the world, that He gave His only begotten Son, that whosoever believeth in Him should not perish, but have everlasting life. John 3:16

Nicodemus came by night. This spiritual leader of Israel did not want anyone to see him talking with the controversial Christ Jesus. Still, he had troubling questions and decided to risk his reputation to have them answered. Nicodemus was a lost soul who found the Master and followed Him.

Nicodemus is mentioned two other times in Scripture: first, when he defended Christ against the unjust suspicions of the Jews (John 7:50), and then later, when he helped to prepare the body of our Lord after His death on the cross (John 19:39). These are strong indications that his belief in the Lord was sincere. Nicodemus had been born again and his life had been forever changed by his faith in Christ Jesus.

John 3:5 teaches that it is necessary to be born again in order to enter God's kingdom. In our first birth, we came out of our mother's womb and became members of our biological family. In our spiritual rebirth, our heart is changed and regenerated as we become part of God's spiritual family.

Prior to becoming a Christian, a person is completely controlled by his old sinful nature. This sinful nature is the spiritual curse that everyone has inherited from Adam. When a person trusts in Christ Jesus, a new nature is added to him. Throughout the rest of the believer's life, the old nature and new nature are in continual conflict with one another. Paul explains this best in Romans 7:15-25, where he talks about the struggle of the two natures within the believer. The Christian may have the desire to do good, but

Born Again

the flesh, being controlled by the sinful nature, wrestles against this Godly desire. It is not until the believer finally gets to heaven that he is rid of the old nature and will be able to serve God in a sinless state. In the meantime, the believer is not condemned in Christ Jesus, for the law of the Spirit of life has set him free from the curse of sin (Romans 8:1-2).

When a person is born again, he has a new capacity and desire to please God. John 14:6 says, "I am the Way, the Truth, and the Life; no man cometh unto the Father, but by Me." Unless we personally accept Jesus Christ as God's Son and place our trust and faith in Him, we have no salvation.

If you have not already done so, seriously consider your relationship with the Lord Jesus Christ. You may have to risk some ridicule like Nicodemus did, but you will quickly discover, as he did, that Christ is the answer to the spiritual void that exists within everyone.

Questions: Please indicate your answer with either True or False.

1. _____ Nicodemus was a Sadducee, a ruler of the Jews. (John 3:1)

2. _____ Nicodemus questioned Jesus about how a man could be born again. (John 3:4)

3. _____ Jesus said that to enter the kingdom of God, a man cannot be born of water and of the Spirit. (John 3:5)

4. _____ Jesus made a distinction between being born of the flesh and being born of the Spirit. (John 3:6)

5. _____ As Moses lifted up the serpent in the wilderness, so must the Son of Man be lifted up. (John 3:14)

6. _____ For God so loved the world that He gave His only begotten Spirit. (John 3:16)

7. _____ God sent His Son into the world to condemn it. (John 3:17)

8. _____ Men love the light rather than the darkness. (John 3:19)

9. _____ Everyone that doeth evil hateth the light. (John 3:20)

10. _____ He that doeth the truth cometh to the light. (John 3:21)

Studying God's Word Book G

Thought Questions:

1. Consider your relationship with God. Are there things that need to be changed? Explain your answer. _____
   _____
   _____
   _____

2. How are the two natures at struggle in your life? _____
   _____
   _____
   _____

Lesson Review:

1. What was the first miracle performed by Jesus? (Lesson #11) _____
   _____

2. How might Satan try to tempt us? (Lesson #10) _____
   _____

3. What was the prophecy foretold in Isaiah 7:14? (Lesson #3) _____
   _____

Supplemental Exercise: Follow the path from start to finish. Count by 7's and connect the numbers. Do not cut across any incorrect numbers.

↓ Start

20	14	21	14	7	14	21	28	35	45	77	84	91	98	105	112	119	126	133	140	147	150
10	13	28	20	14	20	25	35	42	63	70	77	84	91	98	105	588	595	602	610	154	161
49	42	35	34	21	28	35	42	49	56	60	67	73	126	133	140	581	589	609	616	625	168
56	52	54	39	25	29	38	49	55	48	67	88	95	119	154	147	574	580	616	635	182	175
63	71	315	308	301	294	45	56	64	63	74	81	102	112	161	168	567	630	623	642	635	640
70	72	322	329	295	287	52	63	70	77	84	91	98	105	125	175	560	637	630	648	654	647
77	78	343	336	335	280	59	66	245	238	90	97	104	111	118	182	553	644	231	658	651	644
84	349	350	357	360	273	266	259	252	231	224	217	210	203	196	189	546	651	238	665	672	679
91	338	363	364	371	378	385	392	595	588	581	574	567	560	553	546	539	658	665	672	259	686
98	105	112	119	126	133	392	399	434	441	448	455	462	511	518	525	532	665	672	679	266	693
100	107	114	121	128	140	399	406	427	435	448	476	469	504	525	533	707	700	693	686	707	700
107	115	170	165	155	147	406	413	420	442	456	483	490	497	532	715	714	721	728	735	714	721
180	182	175	168	161	154	413	420	427	434	441	462	418	500	539	720	545	566	730	742	750	728
187	189	183	190	197	204	211	218	225	235	448	455	505	510	546	553	560	518	570	749	742	735

↑ Finish

— 39 —

The Woman at the Well
Lesson #13

26 A.D.

Capernaum ■

Sea of Galilee

■ Nazareth

■ Samaria

↑

The region of land between Galilee and Judea is known as Samaria. It is named after its chief city. Traveling through this area Christ met the Samaritan woman.

Jordan River

■ Jerusalem

■ Bethlehem

Dead Sea

0   10   20

Scale of Miles

Lesson Goal: To understand that when it comes to salvation, Christ does not make distinctions upon the basis of wealth or power.

Background Text: John 4:4-42

Memory Verse: God is a Spirit; and they that worship Him must worship Him in spirit and in truth. John 4:24

To the Jews in Christ's time, the Samaritans were considered the lowest form of humanity. If one Jew wanted to insult another, he would call him a Samaritan. This all came about as a result of the Assyrian invasion of the Northern tribe of Israel some 750 years earlier.

Because of the Israelites' disobedience to God, He allowed the Assyrians to capture Israel and take most of the people into captivity. The remaining Jews in the land eventually intermarried with the foreigners from Assyria and became a mixed Jewish race. These "half-breeds" were called Samaritans and were despised by the Jews who had not intermarried with pagans. This hatred was so great that dedicated Jews would not even travel through the land of Samaria, but instead would go the longer way around it.

When Christ walked through Samaria and spoke with the woman at the well, He was breaking down a major cultural barrier. The Samaritans had developed their own system of religion apart from the Jews. They did not follow the

teachings of the Mosaic Law, nor did they go into Jerusalem to worship. The Samaritans had separated themselves from the traditional Jewish religion and culture. It was necessary for Christ to make the point that anyone could believe upon Him. The person's status, color, sex or position did not matter. Anyone could follow the Lord. The Apostle Paul emphasized this message when he said in Galatians 3:28, "There is neither Jew or Greek, there is neither bond nor free, there is neither male or female; for ye are all one in Christ Jesus."

Compare this Samaritan woman to Nicodemus, whom we studied in the previous lesson. Nicodemus was a powerful man with a great deal of influence in the city of Jerusalem. He was a devout Jew who closely followed the teachings of the Law. The Samaritan was a poor woman who was looked down upon even among her own people. She had nothing to offer the Lord except her own sincere belief that He was the Messiah. Still, this woman was like Nicodemus in one unique way: both individuals had to believe upon Christ Jesus for their salvation.

When our Lord says, "Come unto Me all ye that labour and are heavy laden, and I will give you rest" (Matthew 11:28) He is not merely asking for the rich and powerful, the beautiful and strong. Christ is asking anyone who will believe upon Him to come and find spiritual rest for their souls. It does not matter who you are or what you possess. It matters only that you place your trust and faith in the Lord.

Questions:

1. Where is Jacob's well? (John 4:5-6) _____

_____

_____

_____

2. What did Jesus ask of the woman? (John 4:7) _____

_____

_____

_____

3. What type of water did Jesus offer? (John 4:10) _____

_____

4. What did the woman call Jesus? (John 4:19) _____

_____

5. How must we worship God? (John 4:24) _____

_____

6. What question did the disciples ask of Jesus when they saw Him speaking with the Samaritan woman? (John 4:27) _____

_____

The Woman at the Well

7. What did Christ say that His meat was? (John 4:34) _____

_____

8. What did Jesus say concerning the harvest? (John 4:35) _____

_____

9. For how many days did Jesus abide with the Samaritans? (John 4:40) _____

_____

10. What did the Samaritans call Jesus? (John 4:42) _____

_____

Thought Questions:

1. What is one thing that you have in common with Nicodemus and the Samaritan woman? _____

_____

_____

_____

2. What was the cultural barrier that Christ attempted to break down? _____

_____

_____

_____

Lesson Review:

1. Nicodemus met Christ two other times besides the time he asked Jesus how to be born again. What happened in each of those two occasions? (Lesson #12) __

_____

_____

_____

_____

2. Explain how the miracle at Cana was a miracle of quality. (Lesson #11) _____

_____

_____

_____

3. Explain why baptism does not bring salvation. (Lesson #9) _____

_____

_____

_____

A Miracle of Space and Distance
Lesson #14

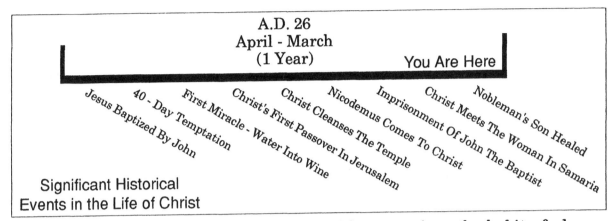

A.D. 26
April - March
(1 Year)
You Are Here

Jesus Baptized By John

40 - Day Temptation

First Miracle - Water Into Wine

Christ's First Passover In Jerusalem

Christ Cleanses The Temple

Nicodemus Comes To Christ

Imprisonment Of John The Baptist

Christ Meets The Woman In Samaria

Nobleman's Son Healed

Significant Historical
Events in the Life of Christ

Lesson Goal: To understand that we should not get into the habit of always asking for things from God, but rather we should ask what we can do for God.

Background Text: John 4:46-54

Memory Verse: Enter into His gates with thanksgiving, and into His courts with praise; be thankful unto Him, and bless His name. Psalm 100:4

This is the second in a series of seven miracles that John describes in order to prove the deity of Christ Jesus. In this passage, John sets forth that Christ has power over space and distance. Our Lord did not need to be right next to a person in order to heal him. He did not need to touch a person in order to remove the disease. It was enough for Christ to will something to happen, and it would be done.

Notice our Lord's response in this passage to not only the official, but also to the people in general. Christ criticized them for not believing in Him unless they saw wonders and miracles. I am afraid that Christians are the same way today. We find ourselves asking more often what God can do for us, than what we can do for Him.

Listen to yourself the next time you pray and count the number of times you ask God for something. It may be specific things, like a new toy or help on a test; or, it could be general things like good health or help to be spiritually strong. Please do not misunderstand. We are supposed to ask God for help, but how often do we ask God what we

A Miracle of Space and Distance

can do for Him? Do we ever thank God for the things He has given us or the times He has helped us in the past?

Let us not fall into the habit of always expecting God to assist us, while neglecting our own responsibilities as Christians. The next time you pray, list the things that God has already done for you and thank Him for them. Then, think of a few ways that you can show your thankfulness and give something back to the Lord in return.

When we pray, we should concentrate upon the four aspects of prayer. We should worship God and give Him our adoration. We need to repent of our sins and confess them to the Lord. We are to give Him thanks and praise for Who He is and what He has done for us. Then finally, we should enter into supplication with our Lord by asking Him for the things that we need, not only for ourselves, but for others as well. A simple way to remember these four parts of prayer are listed below.

Praise   **A**doration
Repent   **C**onfession
Ask (for others, and) **T**hanksgiving
Yourself   **S**upplication

Questions:

1. Jesus came once again into what geographical area? (John 4:46) _____
_____

2. Where did the nobleman's son live? (John 4:46) _____

3. Why did the nobleman seek Jesus? (John 4:47) _____
_____

4. From where was Jesus coming? (John 4:47) _____

5. What did they need to see so that they would believe? (John 4:48) _____
_____

6. Explain how Jesus healed the nobleman's son. (John 4:50) _____
_____

7. What did the servants say to the nobleman? (John 4:51) _____
_____

8. At what hour did the fever leave the son? (John 4:52) _____

9. At what hour did Jesus say, "Thy son liveth"? (John 4:53) _____

10. What was the second miracle that Christ performed? (John 4:54) _____
_____

Thought Questions:

1. Rather than asking something from God, what is something that you can do for God? _____

_____

_____

_____

_____

2. Make a list of several things God has given to you for which you should be thankful. _____

_____

_____

_____

_____

_____

Lesson Review:

1. What was the result of the Assyrian invasion? (Lesson #13) _____

_____

_____

2. Why is it necessary to be born again? (Lesson #12) _____

_____

_____

_____

3. How did Joseph's actions demonstrate a strong belief in the Word of God? (Lesson #4) _____

_____

_____

Supplemental Exercise: Solve the logic problem. (See page 17 for instructions.)

We are familiar with the story of the vineyard owner who went into town to hire laborers for the day's work (Matthew 20). This logic puzzle is about a business owner who hired individuals for different jobs throughout the day. Five times from 9:30 until 12:00, a different individual was hired. From the information given, can you determine each worker's job, the business they work for, and the time they were hired?

A Miracle of Space and Distance

1. Esau went to work for the Lebanon Cedar Co.

2. The brickmaker got a job with Simon's Fishery.

3. The job with Caleb's Camels started at 10:00.

4. Gloria started her job one hour after the carpenter and more than an hour before the person for Sam's Stone Cutters was hired.

5. The Laborer, who was hired at noon, was not Ben.

6. Joseph was hired 90 minutes before the horse seller was hired.

	Carpenter	Brickmaker	Horse Seller	Farmer	Laborer	Caleb's Camels	Simon's Fishery	Sam's Stone Cutters	Jonah's Ship Builders	Lebanon Cedar Co.	9:30	10:00	10:30	11:00	12:00
Judah															
Joseph															
Gloria															
Ben															
Esau															
9:30															
10:00															
10:30															
11:00															
12:00															
Caleb's Camels															
Simon's Fishery															
Sam's Stone Cutters															
Jonah's Ship Builders															
Lebanon Cedar Co.															

Unit Test #1

1. Who was the Word? (John 1:1) _____

2. What did the angel have to tell Zacharias? (Luke 1:13) _____

   _____

3. What happened to Elisabeth when she greeted Mary? (Luke 1:41) _____

   _____

4. What does Emmanuel mean? (Matt. 1:23) _____

5. What was the reaction of those that heard the saying that was told to them by the shepherds? (Luke 2:18) _____

   _____

6. Who served God in the temple where she prayed and fasted night and day? (Luke 2:37) _____

7. What did King Herod tell the wisemen to do? (Matt. 2:8) _____

   _____

8. What was the response of Jesus when Joseph and Mary told Him they were seeking Him? (Luke 2:49) _____

   _____

   _____

9. Where was Jesus baptized? (Matt. 3:13) _____

10. Who descended upon Jesus after He was baptized? (Luke 3:22) _____

    _____

11. If man does not live by bread alone, by what does man live? (Luke 4:4) _____

    _____

12. Who did Satan say would keep charge over Jesus? (Luke 4:10) _____

    _____

13. Why do men love the darkness rather than the light? (John 3:19) _____

    _____

14. How must we worship God? (John 4:24) _____

    _____

15. What was the second miracle that Christ performed? (John 4:54) _____

    _____

A Miracle of Time
Lesson #15

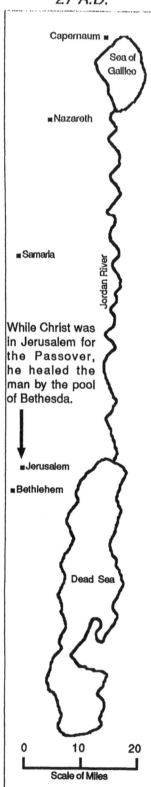

27 A.D.

Capernaum ■

Sea of Galilee

■ Nazareth

■ Samaria

Jordan River

While Christ was in Jerusalem for the Passover, he healed the man by the pool of Bethesda.

■ Jerusalem

■ Bethlehem

Dead Sea

0   10   20

Scale of Miles

Lesson Goal: To understand that bitterness can be worse than a disease or handicap.

Background Text: John 5:1-47

Memory Verse: Looking diligently lest any man fail of the grace of God; lest any root of bitterness springing up trouble you, and thereby many be defiled. Hebrews 12:15

I wish I could take back all of the time I have wasted in my life feeling sorry for myself. Someone, whether accidentally or on purpose, hurts my feelings or bruises my ego, and I mope around all day like I was sick. Does this ever happen to you? No doubt we have all felt sorry for ourselves at one point or another.

In this lesson we find the third miracle recorded by John. In this passage, John shows us that Christ possessed power over time. He healed someone who had been sick for thirty-eight years. This miracle completely restored this man as if he had always been able to walk normally.

Christ asked this man a very unusual question: "Do you wish to get well?" The answer would appear to be obvious. However, could it be that this man was feeling sorry for himself? Was he blaming someone for the fact that he could never make it to the water in time to be cured? Perhaps he was even accusing God for his sickness, thinking that he was a victim of some kind of divine joke. Christ Jesus was asking the man if he had the will and desire to be cured.

How often do we miss the Lord's blessing because we are bitter or feeling sorry for ourselves? Bitterness can rob us of joy and happiness faster than a thief can rob a bank. Perhaps your family has gone through a divorce. Maybe someone close to you has died recently. It could be that you were wrongly accused and judged by someone for something that you did not do. Like the man in this lesson, you may even have a handicap or disease that limits your ability. Whatever is wrong in your life, being bitter and feeling sorry for yourself is not going to make it any better.

Ask yourself: "Do I want to be healed? Do I want to be rid of my bitterness?" Your problem may not go away, but your outlook on life will certainly improve. To paraphrase the Bible for a moment, Christ was saying to the man: forgive and forget, trust in the Lord, pick up your bed and get on with your life. So get on with your life. Leave the bitterness behind and do something productive. To dwell on the problem is only going to make it worse. He has not forgotten you, so trust in the Lord.

Questions: Please indicate your answer with either True or False.

1. _____ There is a pool called Bethseda near the sheep market. (John 5:2)

2. _____ Demons were the ones who troubled the waters of the pool. (John 5:4)

3. _____ The Jews questioned whether it was lawful to heal on the Sabbath day. (John 5:10)

4. _____ The man who was healed did not know Who healed him. (John 5:13)

5. _____ The Jews said that Jesus had made Himself equal with God. (John 5:18)

6. _____ Whoever hears the word of Jesus and believes on Him that sent Jesus hath everlasting life. (John 5:24)

7. _____ God did not give Jesus the authority to execute judgement. (John 5:27)

8. _____ John the Baptist bore witness unto the truth. (John 5:32-33)

9. _____ The Father bore witness of Jesus. (John 5:37)

10. _____ The Scriptures do not bear witness of Jesus. (John 5:39)

A Miracle of Time

<u>Thought Questions</u>:

1. Do you blame anyone for negative things that have happened in your life? Explain your answer. _____

_____

_____

_____

_____

2. How would you advise a person to rid themselves of bitterness? _____

_____

_____

_____

_____

_____

3. How can bitterness hinder a person more than a handicap or disease? _____

_____

_____

_____

_____

_____

<u>Lesson Review</u>:

1. Explain why Christ did not need to be right next to a person in order to heal him. (Lesson #14) _____

_____

_____

_____

2. What is John's purpose in writing like a lawyer? (Lesson #11) _____

_____

_____

_____

3. Why was John reluctant to baptize Jesus? (Lesson #9) _____

_____

_____

_____

At Thy Word
Lesson #16

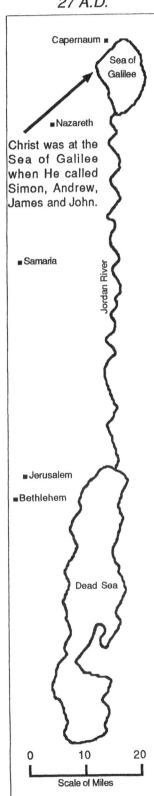

27 A.D.

Capernaum ■

Sea of Galilee

■ Nazareth

Christ was at the Sea of Galilee when He called Simon, Andrew, James and John.

■ Samaria

Jordan River

■ Jerusalem

■ Bethlehem

Dead Sea

0   10   20

Scale of Miles

Lesson Goal: To understand that we are to be obedient to God's Word.

Background Text: Matthew 4:18-22; Mark 1:16-20; Luke 5:1-11

Memory Verse: Now unto Him that is able to do exceeding abundantly above all that we ask or think, according to the power that worketh in us. Ephesians 3:20

How many times do your parents have to ask you to do something before you actually do it? Perhaps you are watching television or reading a book when your mom asks you to take out the garbage. Do you get up right away, or do you wait until she asks you a few more times before you begin moving? I am saddened to say that I was not always the godly example of an obedient child. When my mother asked me to do a chore, there was a certain pitch to her voice that told me how important the job was. I would wait until that pitch was reached in her request before I would get moving. It wasn't until I had children of my own that I began to see how frustrating this can be. As a parent, I do not want to yell at my children, but their sinful nature quickly conditions them not to respond unless they are threatened with punishment. I hope we do not answer to God in the same way that most of us answer to our parents.

Peter's response to our Lord's request was not immediate either. He questioned Christ's authority and was reluctant to cast out his nets. Of course when Peter's nets were filled with fish, he was immediately humbled and ashamed. It is not surprising that he fell before the Lord and proclaimed himself a sinful man.

My friend, God speaks to us through His Word, the Bible. He is telling us things like obey our parents, trust in Christ Jesus and study the Scriptures. How many times does He ask us before we listen and pay attention? How many rich blessings are we missing because we are not immediately obedient to His Word? Imagine what would have happened if Peter had told Christ that he was not going to throw out the net because there was no chance of catching any fish! Not only would he have disobeyed our Lord's command, but he would have also missed seeing a very wonderful miracle performed by Christ Jesus.

Questions: Multiple choice -- circle the correct answer for each question.

1. When Jesus was walking by the sea, who did He see? (Matt. 4:18)
   *Mark and Peter
   *Peter and Simon
   *Peter and Andrew
   *Andrew and Matthew

2. What did Jesus say unto them? (Matt. 4:19)
   *Follow me, and I will make you fishers of men.
   *Blessed are the poor in spirit.
   *Ye are the salt of the earth.
   *Ye are the light of the world.

3. Who were the brothers that were mending their nets? (Matt. 4:21)
   *James and John, the sons of Zorobabel
   *Matthew and Luke, the sons of Zebedee
   *James and John, the sons of Zebedee
   *Mark and Paul, the sons of Ezekiel

4. By what sea did Jesus walk? (Mark 1:16)
   *Dead Sea
   *Mediterranean Sea
   *Sea of Galilee
   *Red Sea

5. By what lake did Jesus stand? (Luke 5:1)
   *Lake Michigan
   *Lake Gennesaret
   *Lake Victoria
   *Lake Gilead

6. What did Jesus ask Simon to do? (Luke 5:3)
   *To go fishing with Him
   *To pray with Him
   *To cook Him something to eat
   *To push his boat a little from the land

7. What was the miracle Jesus performed? (Luke 5:6)
   * *Healed five people of disease
   * *Fed five thousand people
   * *Repaired Simon's net
   * *Allowed a great multitude of fish to be caught

8. What did Simon Peter say when he saw all the fish? (Luke 5:8)
   * *Stay a while and have something to eat.
   * *Depart from me; for I am a sinful man, O Lord.
   * *Depart from us. We do not need your help.
   * *Who art thou that allows this miracle to happen?

9. Instead of fish, what did Jesus say they would catch? (Luke 5:10)
   * *Wisdom
   * *Men
   * *Wealth
   * *Power

10. What did the fishermen do when they came to land? (Luke 5:11)
    * *Forsook all and followed Him
    * *Told Jesus to go away from them
    * *Went back to their homes and gathered their possessions
    * *Got more nets and went back to fish

Thought Questions:

1. In what ways can you be obedient to your parents? _____

   _____

   _____

   _____

2. How can we pay attention to God when He speaks to us? _____

   _____

   _____

   _____

Lesson Review:

1. How did Christ's miracle possess the power over time? (Lesson #15) _____

   _____

   _____

2. Why did Jesus criticize the people? (Lesson #14) _____

   _____

   _____

At Thy Word

3. How could our dreams or desires lead us away from God? (Lesson #6) _____

_____

_____

Supplemental Exercise: Complete the crossword using references from this chapter.

– Across –

1 What they did before they followed Christ (2 words) (Luke 5:11)
5 Present tense of "came"
8 The disciples were to do this to men (Luke 5:10)
9 I will make you become __ of men (Mark 1:17)
11 Christ asked the disciples to do this (Matt. 4:19)
12 Opposite of sister
14 These individuals were in the other boat (Luke 5:7)
16 Another word for amazed (Luke 5:9)
18 What fishermen use to catch fish
21 Jesus asked Simon to thrust out from this (Luke 5:3)
22 Another name for the Sea of Galilee
23 A large body of water
24 James and John were doing this to their nets (Mark 1:19)
26 The occupation of Simon, Andrew, James and John
27 The men were doing this to their nets (Luke 5:2)
28 Simon called Jesus this (Luke 5:5)
30 Who pressed upon Christ (Luke 5:1)
34 This was being done to the net (Matt. 4:18)
35 What did the men do to Christ (Matt. 4:22)
36 Who James and John left (Mark 1:20)

– Down –

2 The opposite of daughters
3 __ of Gennesaret (Luke 5:1)
4 Writer of the 4th Gospel
6 The number of fish the disciples caught (Luke 5:6)
7 Father of James and John
8 Christ did this to Peter and Andrew (Matt. 4:18)
10 Bigger then a boat
13 And going on from there He saw two other __ (Matt. 4:21)
15 When did Christ call the sons of Zebedee (Mark 1:17)
17 When the men left their ship (Matt. 22)
19 The Son of God
20 Opposite of mother
22 Sea of ___.
24 Opposite of women
25 Another name for Christ Jesus
27 Jesus was doing this beside the Sea of Galilee (Matt. 4:18)
29 The brother of Simon
31 The brother ofAndrew
32 The brother of John
33 Another name for Peter

The Boogie Man
Lesson #17

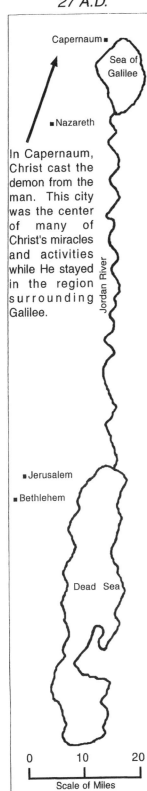

Capernaum ■

Sea of Galilee

■ Nazareth

In Capernaum, Christ cast the demon from the man. This city was the center of many of Christ's miracles and activities while He stayed in the region surrounding Galilee.

Jordan River

■ Jerusalem

■ Bethlehem

Dead Sea

0   10   20

Scale of Miles

Lesson Goal: To understand that God is greater than Satan and the wickedness of the world.

Background Text: Mark 1:23-28; Luke 4:31-37

Memory Verse: For I am persuaded, that neither death, nor life, nor angels, nor principalities, nor powers, nor things present, nor things to come, nor height, nor depth, nor any other creature, shall be able to separate us from the love of God, which is in Christ Jesus our Lord. Romans 8:38-39

As a child, the thought of ghosts frightened me. Even as I grew older, I did not care to walk through a dark room by myself. It sounds silly, but in my mind I never knew if something might jump out and scare me.

We all have fears or things that frighten us. In these lessons, as we study the life of our Lord, we will see how He dealt with the people's fears. Christ taught that He was more powerful than anything that could hinder or hurt His followers. Our memory verse explains that nothing can separate us from the love of God which is in Christ Jesus. That means that no matter what happens to you here on the earth, God's love can never be taken away from you.

We have, in this passage, a glimpse of Christ's power over the spirit world. The demons respected and feared Jesus because they knew that, as the Son of God, He was greater than all of Satan's evil host. This same Christ, Who defeated Satan, indwells His believers through the Holy Spirit.

The Boogie Man

Whenever I become really frightened, I think to myself, "What is the worst possible thing that could happen to me?" Eventually I come up with the answer that I could die a horrible death. Then I think, "Is that really so bad? After all, the moment I die, I will be in heaven." It is amazing that as soon as I rationally deal with my troubles, and recognize that God has supreme power over everything, my fear begins to subside.

We have nothing to fear because beyond death awaits life with our Lord and Savior, Jesus Christ. When Christ died and rose from the dead, He conquered death and hell by providing the means of redemption for His people. We have this promise in I Corinthians 15:55-57, "O death, where is thy sting? O grave, where is thy victory? The sting of death is sin; and the strength of sin is the law. But thanks be to God, which giveth us the victory through our Lord Jesus Christ."

Questions:

1. What did the man in the synagogue have? (Mark 1:23) _____

2. Who did the unclean spirit say Jesus was? (Mark 1:24) _____
_____

3. What did Jesus do to the demons when they announced who Jesus was? (Mark 1:25) _____
_____

4. What did the unclean spirit do? (Mark 1:26) _____
_____

5. What was the response of the people who saw this miracle? (Mark 1:27) _____
_____
_____

6. Who did the unclean spirits obey? (Mark 1:27) _____

7. Throughout what area did the news spread? (Mark 1:28) _____
_____

8. What happened to the man when the devil came out of him? (Luke 4:35) _____
_____

9. On what days did Jesus teach? (Luke 4:31) _____

10. Where was Jesus when He taught? (Luke 4:31) _____

_____

Thought Questions:

1. What do you fear the most? Explain your answer. _____

_____

_____

_____

_____

2. How can God help you through your fears? _____

_____

_____

_____

_____

Lesson Review:

1. Explain Peter's obedience concerning the Lord's request to lower the nets into

the sea. (Lesson #16) _____

_____

_____

2. For how many years had the man been sick and unable to walk? (Lesson #15)

_____

3. Who revealed to Simeon that Jesus was God's Son? (Lesson #6) _____

_____

> *Cowards die many times*
> *before their deaths;*
> *The valiant never taste*
> *of death but once.*
> *Shakespeare, Julius Caesar, II,2*

Matthew Background

<u>Author of Matthew</u>: Matthew, also called Levi. His occupation was a tax collector before Christ called him to be a disciple (Matt. 9:9; Mark 2:14; Luke 5:27).

<u>Date of Writing</u>: Around 50 A.D.

<u>Purpose of Matthew</u>: To demonstrate that Christ was the rightful heir to the Abrahamic and Davidic covenants, and to present Jesus Christ as the King of Israel in exact fulfillment of the Old Testament prophecies.

<u>Outline of Matthew</u>:

I. The Birth and Childhood of the King (Matt. 1 & 2)
    A. Genealogy of Christ (1:1-17)
    B. Birth of Christ (1:18-25)
    C. Visit of the Magi (2:1-12)
    D. Flight into Egypt (2:13-18)
    E. Residence at Nazareth (2:19-23)

II. The Beginnings of the King (3:1-4:11)
    A. The Forerunner of Christ (3:1-12)
    B. Baptism of Christ (3:12-17)
    C. Temptation of Christ (4:1-11)

III. The Ministry of the King (Matt. 4:12-25:46)
    A. In Galilee (4:12-18:35)
        1. His Followers (4:12-4:25)
        2. His Message (Matt. 5-7)
        3. His Power and Authority (Matt. 8-10)
        4. His Opposition (Matt. 11 & 12)
        5. His Parables (Matt. 13)
        6. His Instruction (Matt. 14-18)
    B. In Judea (Matt. 19 & 20)
        1. His Teaching (19:1-20:16)
        2. His Interaction (20:17-34)
    C. In Jerusalem (Matt. 21-25)
        1. His Presentation (21:1-22)
        2. His Rejection (21:23-23:39)
        3. His Prophecy (Matt. 24 & 25)

IV. The Passion of the King (Matt. 26 & 27)
    A. His Annointing (26:1-13)
    B. His Passover (26:14-30)

C. His Agony (26:31-46)
D. His Arrest (26:47-56)
E. His Trials (26:57-27:26)
F. His Crucifixion (27:27-56)
G. His Burial (27:57-66)

V. The Resurrection of the King (Matt. 28)
  A. The Events (28:1-15)
  B. The Commission (28:16-20)

Big Idea of Matthew: The early church fathers taught that the Book of Matthew was written to converts from Judaism. Matthew used fulfilled prophecy to bridge the gap of understanding between the Old Testament and God's new spiritual family, the church. Matthew demonstrated that the Old Testament sacrificial system was fulfilled through the death and resurrection of the Lord Jesus Christ. Christ Jesus had come to the people as their Messiah to atone for their sins once and for all.

Matthew also presents Christ as the Son of David and the Son of Abraham. Using the genealogy of Joseph (Matt. 1:1-17), Matthew traces the line of Christ back to Abraham through the royal line of David. Compare this to Luke who traces Christ's family back to Adam through the priestly line of Aaron. Matthew presents Christ as the King of Israel; whereas, Luke presents Christ as the High Priest of Israel.

The word "Kingdom" appears over fifty times in Matthew, and "Kingdom of Heaven" appears over thirty times. Matthew emphasizes the concept of Christ as the King of Israel and explains how we, as His subjects, are to live and act in His kingdom.

Matthew gives a great amount of detail to the sermons of Christ Jesus. Seven of our Lord's sermons are presented in the book.

The Sermon on the Mount (5:1-7:29)
Commission of the Twelve Disciples (10:1-42)
Parables of the Kingdom (13:1-52)
Humility and Forgiveness (18:1-35)
Condemnation of Hypocrisy (23:1-36)
The Olivet Discourse (24:3-25:46)
The Great Commission (28:16-20)

Approximately 42% of the Gospel of Matthew is unique to the other three gospels.

Through the Roof
Lesson #18

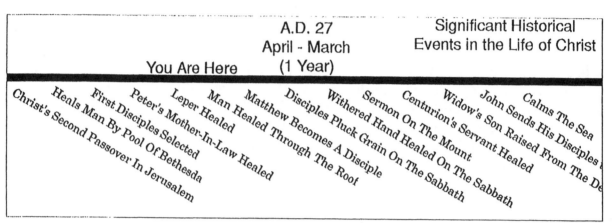

Christ's Second Passover In Jerusalem — Heals Man By Pool Of Bethesda — First Disciples Selected — Peter's Mother-In-Law Healed — Leper Healed — Man Healed Through The Roof — Matthew Becomes A Disciple — Disciples Pluck Grain On The Sabbath — Withered Hand Healed On The Sabbath — Sermon On The Mount — Centurion's Servant Healed — Widow's Son Raised From The De... — John Sends His Disciples... — Calms The Sea

Lesson Goal: To understand that Christ is God's Son.

Background Text: Matthew 9:2-8; Mark 2:1-12; Luke 5:17-26

Memory Verse: In the beginning was the Word, and the Word was with God, and the Word was God. John 1:1

When we think about roofs these days, we normally think about "A-frame" style homes, where the roof goes up at an angle and meets at a point. This was not the case during the time when Christ lived. The houses then had flat roofs, made with stone, baked mud or straw. Most often, they were strong enough to walk on, with stairs leading to them from the lower levels. This provided extra living space for the occupants. With this in mind, the men in this lesson were able to dig up the roof and lower their friend down to Jesus.

It is important to understand a conflict developing among the people toward Christ. It was eventually this conflict that led to our Lord's crucifixion. Christ had become very popular because the people saw Him as a miracle-worker and healer. What they did not expect to find was someone Who could also forgive sin. This caused the religious leaders much distress since they refused to believe that Jesus was God's Son.

Our Lord condemned the selfish interests of the scribes and Pharisees because they wanted to control the religious thinking of the people. Christ called these leaders "hypocrites" because they instructed the people to live by petty, man-

made regulations, and discouraged them from seeking true faith and belief in God. For example, the Pharisees would wear on their foreheads tiny boxes with Scripture references tucked inside. This practice developed from a literal interpretation of Exodus 13:9-16. In this passage, the Jews were commanded to keep God's Word close to their hearts and minds. Their legalistic ritual replaced what God intended for the people to do through memorization and meditation in the Scriptures.

As the religious leaders purposed to destroy Christ, they formed mobs to kill Him and they tried to trick Him with leading questions. Of course, their plans and attempts were frustrated until Christ allowed Himself to be captured and crucified.

It is easy for us to be critical of these people because they did not believe in Christ as God's Son. We tend to think that it was obvious for them to see that Christ was the Messiah because of all the miracles He performed. However, before we become too judgmental, look around and see how many people actually believe in Christ today. Unfortunately, even now, people will find all kinds of excuses not to entrust their lives to the Lord Jesus as their Savior.

Questions: Please indicate your answer with either True or False.

1. _____ Jesus said to the paralyzed man that his sins were forgiven. (Matt. 9:2)

2. _____ The Pharisees said that Jesus blasphemed. (Matt. 9:3)

3. _____ Jesus said that the Son of Man has power on earth to forgive sins. (Matt. 9:6)

4. _____ The paralyzed man did not rise up and go to his house. (Matt. 9:7)

5. _____ There were so many who wanted to see Jesus that they had to stand in front of the door of the house. (Mark 2:2)

6. _____ The friends of the paralyzed man lowered him through the roof because of the crowd. (Mark 2:4)

7. _____ Jesus perceived that the scribes reasoned in their hearts against Him. (Mark 2:6-8)

8. _____ When the people saw this miracle, they were amazed and glorified God. (Mark 2:12)

9. _____ The Pharisees and the doctors of the law came out of every town of Galilee, Samaria and Jerusalem. (Luke 5:17)

10. _____ The power of the Lord was present in Jesus to heal the sick. (Luke 5:17)

Through the Roof

<u>Thought Questions</u>:

1. How can you avoid being a hypocrite? _____

_____

_____

_____

2. Why do you think people find it difficult to trust their lives to the Lord Jesus? List a few excuses. _____

_____

_____

_____

<u>Lesson Review</u>:

1. How did Christ demonstrate that He was greater than Satan's host? (Lesson #17) _____

_____

_____

2. Where did Christ heal the nobleman's son? (Lesson #14) _____

_____

3. In Christ's third recorded temptation, what did the devil say he would give Him? (Lesson #10) _____

_____

<u>Supplemental Exercise</u>: Fill in the Scrabble crossword below with the names of the twelve disciples. Where more than one name is recorded for a disciple, all have been included in this puzzle. The first disciple has been given to help you start. For assistance refer to Matt. 10:2-4, Mark 3:16-19, Luke 6:13-16, John 1:45.

Too Sinful for God?
Lesson #19

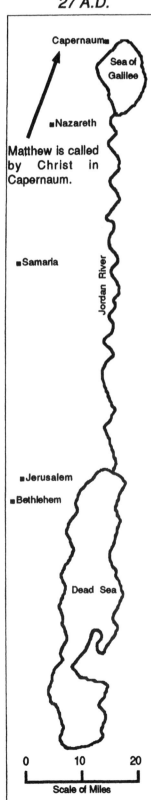

27 A.D.

Capernaum

Sea of Galilee

Nazareth

Matthew is called by Christ in Capernaum.

Samaria

Jordan River

Jerusalem

Bethlehem

Dead Sea

0   10   20

Scale of Miles

<u>Lesson Goal</u>: To understand that no sin is too great for God to forgive.

<u>Background Text</u>: Matthew 9:9-13; Mark 2:13-17; Luke 5:27-32

<u>Memory Verse</u>: I came not to call the righteous, but sinners to repentance. Luke 5:32

In Biblical times, the Jewish people hated tax collectors. Not only did they take the taxes from the people, but most of them were also liars and cheats. Christ made it a practice to go to the most outwardly sinful people, which included tax collectors, because they were open to His message. They did not have any preconceived ideas about religion like the Pharisees had. In fact, they had been rejected and outcast by the religious elite because of their sinful practices. Christ, by reaching out to these sinful people, was teaching that God extends His forgiveness to them as well. Those who were self-righteous did not recognize their need for God because they felt that they had no need for a Savior.

There are people in the world today who believe that they have committed such terrible acts of unrighteousness that God would never truly forgive and accept them. This is simply not true. When an individual becomes a Christian, he is immediately accepted by God into His holy family and has his sins forgiven. Now, he may still have to pay the earthly consequences of his sin; however, in the eyes of God, his sins are washed away and his heart is cleansed.

When King David sinned by committing adultery and murder (II Samuel 11-20), although he was forgiven by God, he was still accountable for the consequences of his sins. These consequences manifested themselves years later when David's son, Amnon, raped his half-sister Tamar; Amnon was murdered by Absalom; and Absalom attempted to lead a rebellion to overthrow the government of his father, King David.

It is comforting to know that we can come to Christ, regardless of what we have done, and be reconciled with God. As Christians, we are not to use this as an excuse to continue to sin, but rather as a means of glorifying God by serving Him. As David's life illustrated, sin can be very destructive; but to the repentant sinner, God's forgiveness covers everything.

Questions:

1. Who did Jesus call to become His disciple? (Matt. 9:9) _____
_____

2. Who came and sat with Jesus and His disciples in the house? (Matt. 9:10) ____
_____

3. What did the Pharisees say to the disciples when they saw who was eating with Jesus? (Matt. 9:11) _____
_____
_____

4. Who are the ones that need a physician? (Matt. 9:12) _____
_____

5. Who did Jesus come to call? (Matt. 9:13) _____
_____

6. Where did Jesus teach the multitude? (Mark 2:13) _____
_____

7. What was the name of the man who Jesus called to become His disciple? (Mark 2:14) _____

8. What was Levi's occupation? (Luke 5:27) _____

9. What did Levi do for Jesus? (Luke 5:29) _____
_____

10. Besides Jesus and His disciples, who else was at Levi's house? (Luke 5:29) __
_____

<u>Thought Questions</u>:

1. Do you feel that you can do whatever you want because you know that God will forgive you? Explain your answer. _____

_____

_____

_____

2. Why do you think some people have a difficult time believing that God can forgive them for their sins? _____

_____

_____

_____

<u>Lesson Review</u>:

1. Why did Jesus call the Jewish officials hypocrites? (Lesson #18) _____

_____

_____

2. How many husbands did the Samaritan woman have? (Lesson #13) _____

3. Where did the feast of the Passover take place? (Lesson #8) _____

_____

<u>Supplemental Exercise</u>: Complete the puzzle and find the hidden phrase.

And after these things He went forth, and saw a [1], named Levi, sitting at the receipt of custom; and He said unto him, [9] Me. And he left all, [7] up, and followed Him. And Levi made Him a [6] feast in his own house; and there was a great [8] of publicans and of others that sat down with them. But the Pharisees and their scribes [10] against his disciples, saying, "Why do ye eat and [4] with publicans and sinners?" And Jesus, answering, said unto them, "They that are whole need not a physician, but they that are sick. I came not to call the [2] but [3] to [5]. (Luke 5:27-32)

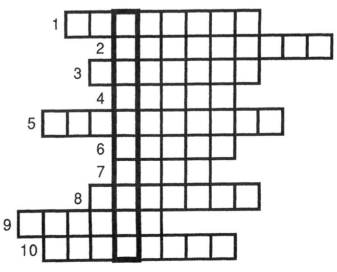

Commitment or Sacrifice
Lesson #20

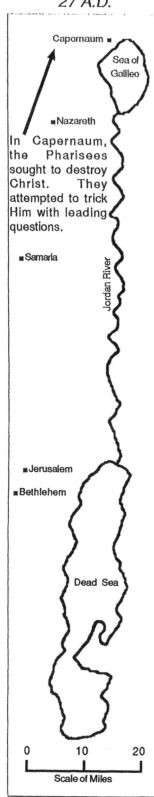

27 A.D.

Capernaum ■

Sea of Galilee

■ Nazareth

In Capernaum, the Pharisees sought to destroy Christ. They attempted to trick Him with leading questions.

■ Samaria

Jordan River

■ Jerusalem

■ Bethlehem

Dead Sea

0   10   20

Scale of Miles

Lesson Goal: To understand that God desires a pure heart, not merely the appearance of righteousness.

Background Text: Matthew 12:1-14; Mark 2:23-3:6; Luke 6:1-11

Memory Verse: I beseech you therefore, brethren, by the mercies of God, that ye present your bodies a living sacrifice, holy, acceptable unto God, which is your reasonable service. Romans 12:1

The Pharisees had a practice of adding legalistic rules and requirements to the Law of Moses. They were more concerned with following the letter of the Law than they were in understanding its intended meaning and purpose. We have two examples in this lesson in which the Pharisees accused Jesus and His disciples of working on the Sabbath and thereby sinning against the Law. The Pharisees had a greater desire to appear holy than to actually have a holy heart. Christ and His disciples did not sin on the Sabbath, but that did not matter to the Pharisees since they were trying to trick our Lord.

It is sometimes easy to go through the motions of being a Christian in order to appear righteous, without truly believing in the things we do. We may go to church, read our Bible, and pray before meals, but are we doing these things because we have to or because we want to? When our parents ask us to do a task, do we do it grumbling or do we do it graciously? Sometimes, what we do is not as important as our motivation for doing it.

It is God's desire that we love and serve Him with a pure heart, not to simply go through the motions of looking good. God told the children of Israel that He wanted commitment, not sacrifice. He was saying to them that He was not directly interested in the sacrificing of an animal on the altar. God wanted their hearts to be pure so that through the sacrifice and the service of worship, they would be drawn into a closer relationship with Him.

Studying God's Word Book G

The Apostle Paul repeated this same message in Romans 12:1. Here he admonished the believers to present themselves to God as holy sacrifices. We are not to become so caught up in the trappings of legalism that we lose sight of our true objective. Appearances do not make a person holy. A pure heart, committed to God, makes a person holy.

Questions:

1. Jesus and His disciples went through the _____ on the _____ day. (Matt. 12:1)

2. The _____ saw it and told the _____ that it was _____ to do on the _____ day. (Matt. 12:2)

3. _____ told them the example of the time when _____ was _____. (Matt. 12:3)

4. _____ went into the _____ to eat the _____ which was not _____ for him to eat. (Matt. 12:3-4)

5. Jesus said that in this place there is _____ greater than the _____. (Matt. 12:6)

6. The _____ was made for _____, and not _____ for the _____. (Mark 2:27)

7. The _____ is Lord over the _____. (Mark 2:28)

8. Jesus entered the _____ and there was a man with a _____ hand. (Mark 3:1)

9. The _____ and the _____ watched to see if Jesus would heal the man on the _____. (Luke 6:7)

– 67 –

Commitment or Sacrifice

10. Jesus asked whether it was lawful on the Sabbath days to do _____ or to do _____? To save _____ or to _____ it? (Luke 6:9)

Thought Questions:

1. What should your motivation be when you go to church, read the Bible or pray? _____

_____

_____

_____

2. How can you demonstrate your commitment to God every day? _____

_____

_____

_____

3. What can you do to improve your attitude about the Lord and the things of His Word? _____

_____

_____

Lesson Review:

1. Why did the Jewish people hate the tax collectors? (Lesson #19) _____

_____

_____

2. Who were the brothers that were mending their nets when Christ called them? (Lesson #16) _____

_____

3. Who was to bear witness of the Light? (Lesson #1) _____

_____

Happiness Is. . .
Lesson #21

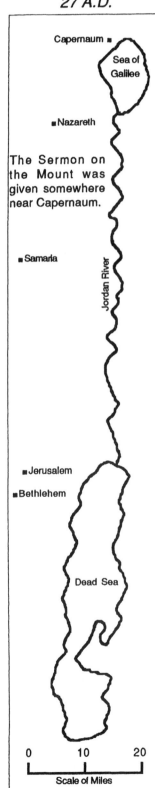

27 A.D.

Capernaum

Sea of Galilee

Nazareth

The Sermon on the Mount was given somewhere near Capernaum.

Samaria

Jordan River

Jerusalem

Bethlehem

Dead Sea

0   10   20

Scale of Miles

Lesson Goal: To understand what it means to be citizens of God's kingdom.

Background Text: Matthew 5:1-16

Memory Verse: Let your light so shine before men, that they may see your good works, and glorify your Father which is in heaven. Matthew 5:16

Many of the goals of these lessons center on such themes as the believer's character, following God's will, leading a righteous life and practicing Godliness. Regardless of what we call them, all these areas of Christian conduct focus upon one question: How does our Lord desire the believer to live in a pagan and sinful world? Christ answers that question in this passage of Scripture commonly known as the "Sermon on the Mount." Its theme does not address the issue of salvation, but rather how the believer is to live and act in God's kingdom.

Since so many books have already been written on this passage of Scripture, we are going to cover it in four separate lessons. This should give you a brief overview of the text, so you can delve into further concentrated study in your own time. No other passage of Scripture has had such a profound impact upon my spiritual life as these three chapters from Matthew's Gospel. While I was in the tenth grade, I committed these chapters to memory and have treasured them in my heart ever since. In this first lesson, we are going to concentrate upon what it means to be citizens of Christ's kingdom.

There is much confusion in society today about happiness. Everyone seems to seek it, but not many people appear to obtain it. There is nothing wrong with the believer being happy, but if we seek after happiness alone, our priorities will become confused.

True happiness is not an emotion we strive or work toward, but rather it is a result of the believer following God's will and receiving His blessing. Christ explains happiness in

Happiness Is...

this way, "Blessed [or happy] are the poor in spirit; for their's is the Kingdom of Heaven. Blessed [or happy] are they that mourn; for they shall be comforted." (Matthew 5:3-4) Our Lord goes on to describe several conditions that can bring a person happiness in God's kingdom.

Citizens of God's kingdom include individuals who are gentle, merciful, pure in heart, and even persecuted. Now how can a person be happy when persecuted? Persecution generally involves pain, and pain does not make many people happy. The persecuted believer is happy because he knows that he is living for God's kingdom. There is a sense of satisfaction and confidence that the Christian develops when he serves the Lord with a pure heart. We do not need to seek happiness because it is something that we cannot attain by itself. Happiness will come as a result of living for the Lord as citizens of His kingdom.

<u>Questions</u>: Match the correct answer with the proper question.

1. _____ Blessed are the poor in spirit, for what is their's? (Matt. 5:3)

2. _____ Blessed are they that mourn, for what shall they be? (Matt. 5:4)

3. _____ Blessed are the meek, for what shall they do? (Matt. 5:5)

4. _____ Blessed are they which hunger and thirst after righteousness, for what shall they be? (Matt. 5:6)

5. _____ Blessed are the merciful, for what shall they obtain? (Matt. 5:7)

6. _____ Blessed are the pure in heart, for what shall they see? (Matt. 5:8)

7. _____ Blessed are the peacemakers, for what shall they be called? (Matt. 5:9)

8. _____ What are the believers called? (Matt. 5:13)

9. _____ What is set on a hill that cannot be hid? (Matt. 5:14)

10. _____ What do you not put under a bushel? (Matt. 5:15)

a. Inherit the earth

b. Mercy

c. Filled

d. A candle

e. Salt of the earth

f. Kingdom of heaven

g. The children of God

h. A city

i. Comforted

j. God

Happiness is in the heart, not in the circumstances.

Thought Questions:

1. What would you consider to be true happiness? _____

_____

_____

2. How can you turn a bad situation in your life to something that is profitable?

_____

_____

_____

Lesson Review:

1. What did the Pharisees have a practice of doing? (Lesson #20) _____

_____

2. Who were the first four disciples called by Jesus? (Lesson #16) _____

_____

_____

3. Explain how Christ's first miracle was a miracle of quality. (Lesson #11) _____

_____

_____

Supplemental Exercise: Find and circle the words listed in the word search puzzle. Words may be forward, backward, horizontal, vertical or diagonal.

MULTITUDES	MOURN	
POOR IN SPIRIT	MEEK	
COMFORTED	INHERIT	
KINGDOM	HUNGER	
THIRST	FILLED	
RIGHTEOUS	MERCIFUL	
PURE IN HEART	MERCY	
PEACEMAKERS	REJOICE	
PERSECUTED	REWARD	
SALT	GLAD	
SAVOR	EARTH	
TRODDEN	LIGHT	
BUSHEL	SHINE	
GLORIFY	FATHER	
CANDLESTICK	HILL	
CANDLE	HOUSE	
MEN	WORKS	
CHILDREN OF GOD		

```
W R E I N I E K G U D O J H T E E R A
K L D G A N O S S E C I O J E R R N I
M R D P H O D A L F S O D W D U Y E C
S E D U T I T L U M R E M O R G F H L
I G R B R E I T F O T D T R C A I M P
Q N I E A F R K I U R A E K N B R D E
S U G I E O I O C R A K L S A V O R L
R H H F D N P E R N E E E Z U G L A D
E Z T D G Y S C E E H H B U F O G W N
K A E D Z R N V M S N W N O A T H E A
A N O U E A I E U O I U N I T Y I R C
M M U P D A R B M G E E H O H S L L B
E A S L I C O M F O R T E D E A L T E
C R E L Y U O A E D U L E N R P S O R
A N S I S O P H L V P X T N T R Q O T
E W S H I N E I N M T T H G I L A S A
P U E L L R H B O F T I K H S S K B R
L N V J E C A N D L E S T I C K E N L
```

A New Kind of Law
Lesson #22

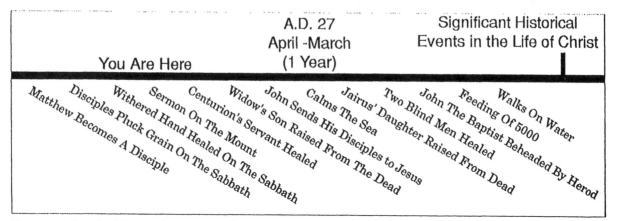

You Are Here	A.D. 27 April -March (1 Year)	Significant Historical Events in the Life of Christ

Matthew Becomes A Disciple
Disciples Pluck Grain On The Sabbath
Withered Hand Healed On The Sabbath
Sermon On The Mount
Centurion's Servant Healed
Widow's Son Raised From The Dead
John Sends His Disciples to Jesus
Calms The Sea
Jairus' Daughter Raised From Dead
Two Blind Men Healed
John The Baptist Beheaded By Herod
Feeding Of 5000
Walks On Water

Lesson Goal: To understand the guidelines of living in God's kingdom.

Background Text: Matthew 5:17-48

Memory Verse: Be ye therefore perfect, even as your Father which is in heaven is perfect. Matthew 5:48

Laws can be divided into two categories, temporal laws and absolute laws. Temporal laws are laws that will change from time to time. For example, the 55-mile-per-hour speed limit, and many city and village zoning requirements, are temporal laws. Absolute laws are moral laws that were originally established by God and never change. The Ten Commandments are examples of God's absolute moral laws.

In this section, Christ explains to His disciples that attitudes are just as important as actions. In the kingdom of God, we are no longer condemned by the Law because the grace of Christ has set us free. This does not mean that we can willfully disobey God's laws, but rather that we fulfill them with righteous attitudes.

Our Lord illustrates this principle by explaining how God's absolute law is fulfilled by the righteous attitudes of the citizens of His kingdom. God's moral law tells us not to commit murder. Christ expands upon this by saying that in addition to not committing murder, a believer is not even to become unjustly angry with his brother. In another example, Christ teaches that instead of hating your enemy, you are to love him.

The purpose of this teaching was to prove a point to His listeners. They were living by the false assumption that all they needed to do was to obey the Law, that it was their outward actions that God deemed significant. As the people outwardly abided by God's moral absolutes, inwardly their hearts were full of anger, strife, malice and envy. Christ was pointing a finger at the people and saying, "Stop it!" In the kingdom of God, what you think in your heart is just as important as

what you do with your hands. Ultimately, it is the attitudes of your heart that determine the actions of your life.

The application to us, as believers, is quite evident. We need to cultivate the kind of attitudes that will produce righteous actions. God does not want us to follow a list of man-made "do's and don't's" with no regard to our commitment to the Lord. What we do will be a natural outgrowth of what we think and believe. If we hate our brother, we will demonstrate that hatred by showing anger and malice toward him. On the other hand, if we love our brother, our love will be demonstrated toward him in the form of kindness, compassion, and forgiveness. As citizens of God's kingdom, the law by which we live should be the absolute Law of God written within our hearts.

Questions: Please indicate your answer with either True or False.

1. _____ Jesus came to destroy the Law. (Matt. 5:17)

2. _____ Our righteousness must exceed the righteousness of the scribes and Pharisees. (Matt. 5:20)

3. _____ Whosoever is angry with his brother without a cause shall be in danger of the judgement. (Matt. 5:22)

4. _____ You must make things right with your brother before you can go and offer your gift at the alter. (Matt. 5:24)

5. _____ It is better that one part of your body perish than for your whole body to be thrown into hell. (Matt. 5:29)

6. _____ It has been said that in order to put away your wife you need to lock her in a closet. (Matt. 5:31)

7. _____ If someone hits you on the cheek, turn to him the other. (Matt. 5:39)

8. _____ If someone wants you to go a mile, go with him three miles. (Matt. 5:41)

9. _____ Love your enemies hate them that curse you and pray for them that care for you. (Matt. 5:44)

10. _____ The Father makes the sun to rise on the evil and the good. (Matt. 5:45)

A New Kind of Law

<u>Thought Questions</u>:

1. How do the attitudes of your heart show what your actions will be? _____

_____

_____

_____

2. In God's kingdom, are the things that we believe just as important as the things that we do? Explain your answer. _____

_____

_____

_____

<u>Lesson Review</u>:

1. What will the persecuted receive for righteousness sake? (Lesson #21) _____

_____

2. Who was the Pharisee that went to talk with Jesus by night? (Lesson #12) ___

_____

3. Explain why Adam did not have complete knowledge even while in his sinless state. (Lesson #8) _____

_____

<u>Supplemental Exercise</u>: Most of the New Testament was orginally written in the Greek language. It is from these early manuscripts that we translate our version of the Bible. Note that the Greek language may sound choppy to those of you accustomed to the English, but the meaning is still the same. Since this is a basic word-for-word translation, English grammar rules are not being used.

Translate this Greek passage from John 1:1 into English. The dictionary can be found in Appendix C.

εν αρχη ην ο λογος

_____

και ο λογος ην προς τον θεον

_____

και θεος ην ο λογος

_____

Practices of the Kingdom
Lesson #23

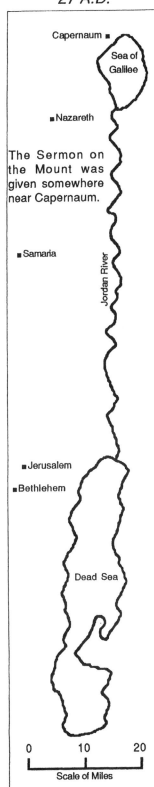

27 A.D.

Capernaum ■

Sea of Galilee

■ Nazareth

The Sermon on the Mount was given somewhere near Capernaum.

■ Samaria

Jordan River

■ Jerusalem

■ Bethlehem

Dead Sea

0   10   20

Scale of Miles

Lesson Goal: To understand the basis of spiritual living in God's kingdom.

Background Text: Matthew 6:1-7:12

Memory Verse: Ask, and it shall be given you; seek, and ye shall find; knock, and it shall be opened unto you. Matthew 7:7

How do our activities in God's kingdom affect our lives and the lives of everyone around us? Do we practice the principles of righteousness in a vacuum, or is there purpose to the things that we do and believe? When the fog is thickest before our eyes and the mist rolls beneath our feet, it is then that God's Word comes to us like a beacon, cutting through the haze and darkness to illuminate the path beneath us. Our wisdom lies in the ability to see the light before our feet and follow the path of righteousness.

In God's kingdom, our Lord gives us specific instructions as to how we are to act in relation to ourselves and others. Our spiritual commitment is not to be exhibited before men so as to gain their praise and admiration, but in secret before God. Whether we fast, pray or give an offering, our motivation should not be the praise of men but the glory of God.

The good works that we perform on earth will have eternal value in heaven. We are not to concentrate our efforts on increasing our material wealth upon the earth. Treasure which is laid up in heaven will have value that will last for eternity. So which would you rather have: a million dollars that will last for about seventy years, or unlimited wealth that will last for eternity?

Someone will say in reply, "I am poor. I have to worry about feeding and clothing my family!" No, worry is not acceptable behavior in God's kingdom. God will provide for His righteous followers in ways that would seem impossible to man. We still have our responsibilities. We need to work and remain faithful to God. It is not as if we sit at home and wait for God to provide bread for our meal by dropping it on our door step. When we seek first God's kingdom, He will provide for our physical needs, not merely our spiritual ones.

In God's kingdom, we are to act towards others in a way that would honor our Lord. We are not to unjustly judge our brother or be unnecessarily critical of him. We all have sin which is evident in our lives. Oftentimes, we are critical of the very same sins in others that we have in ourselves. Instead of judging our brother, we are to help him overcome his sin while at the same time helping ourselves to overcome our own sin.

We are also not to be naive about the wicked actions of men. Certain individuals who may have the outward appearance of Christians will try to lead true believers away from the Gospel of our Lord. Christ calls these individuals wolves. They think only of their own selfish interests, with no regard to the building up of the body of Christ.

This section of Scripture contains many practical guidelines to assist us in our daily spiritual pilgrimage. By our careful study and commitment of this text to memory, we will have a guide that will assist us in the decisions that we make for the rest of our lives.

Questions:

1. What are you not to do before men? (Matt. 6:1) _____

_____

_____

2. What do the hypocrites do when they pray? (Matt. 6:5) _____

_____

3. Where are we supposed to go when we pray? (Matt. 6:6) _____

_____

4. What are we not supposed to use when we pray? (Matt. 6:7) _____

_____

5. What are we to do when we fast? (Matt. 6:17) _____

_____

6. Where are we to lay our treasures? (Matt. 6:20) _____

7. What are we to seek first? (Matt. 6:33) _____
   _____

8. Why should we not judge others? (Matt. 7:1-2) _____
   _____

9. What are we not to cast before swine? (Matt. 7:6) _____

10. What are we not to give dogs? (Matt. 7:6) _____

Thought Questions:

1. How do your actions affect others around you? _____
   _____
   _____
   _____
   _____

2. How should your spiritual commitment to God be exhibited? _____
   _____
   _____
   _____
   _____

Lesson Review:

1. Explain the difference between temporal and absolute laws. (Lesson #22) ____
   _____
   _____
   _____

2. What was the purpose of the Book of Matthew? (Matthew Background) _____
   _____
   _____
   _____

3. Why was it necessary for Jesus to be baptized? (Lesson #9) _____
   _____
   _____
   _____

Living in the Kingdom
Lesson #24

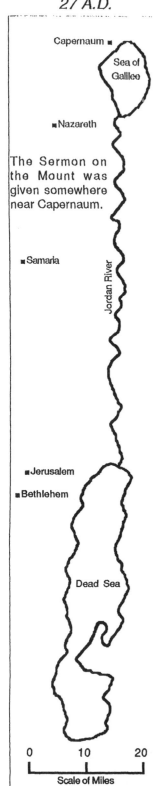

27 A.D.

Capernaum ■

Sea of Galilee

■Nazareth

The Sermon on the Mount was given somewhere near Capernaum.

■Samaria

Jordan River

■Jerusalem

■Bethlehem

Dead Sea

0   10   20

Scale of Miles

Lesson Goal: To understand the result of living in God's kingdom.

Background Text: Matthew 7:21-29

Memory Verse: Therefore whosoever heareth these sayings of mine, and doeth them, I will liken him unto a wise man which built his house upon a rock. Matthew 7:24

Like so many good teachers, our Lord ended His sermon with an illustration. Most of us have probably heard it before, and have even sung about it in Sunday school. The person who hears the words of Christ, and acts upon them, is like a wise man who builds his house upon a rock.

Any good builder or contractor will tell you that a strong foundation is necessary in building a secure structure. Sand and mud will move and shift over the passing of time. If a building is erected on soft soil, it will slowly sink into the earth. Whether it be a home, warehouse, or office building, if the foundation is bad, the rest of the structure will eventually fall apart.

Christ likens this illustration to our spiritual lives. A smart contractor will build a house upon a solid foundation because rock will not slide or move as easily as dirt or sand will. For the believer, this solid foundation is the Lord Jesus Christ and His Word. When we base our lives upon God's Word and act in accordance with its teachings, we are not going to get knocked down or defeated when trials come our way. James 1:6 stresses the same point: "But let him ask in faith, nothing wavering. For he that wavereth is like a wave of the sea driven with the wind and tossed." A person who does not trust the Word of our Lord is like the waves of the sea. He will be unable to control what happens to him because he has no anchor or foundation. Therefore, when trials come against him, he will be knocked down, blown away, and defeated.

As citizens of God's kingdom, we need to abide by His absolute moral standards. More specifically, we need to apply the Sermon on the Mount to our everyday lives. Society today teaches that there are no absolute standards. Therefore, most people live by their own set of humanistic guidelines with no basis for them from God's Word. For example, humanism teaches that man evolved from apes and survived in life by becoming the most intelligent of the creatures. This "survival of the fittest" mentality becomes the basis of man's ethical structure. As a result, a person can say I am stronger or smarter than another person and can do whatever I please to him. What has happened is that society has based its thinking, and way of living, upon this faulty humanistic value.

These values, taken to their logical conclusion, give society the moral dilemmas of abortion, in-vitro fertilization, child abuse, euthanasia, organ farms, etc. A child is aborted because someone says that they do not want to be inconvenienced, that their life is more valuable than the child's life. Children are abused because man's irrational values tell them, "If I can kill a child, why can't I beat him up?" The sick and elderly are either left to die, or are put to sleep like an old dog, because they have no "value" to society and have become a financial burden to the rest of us. Eventually we will have organ farms, where unborn babies are grown in test tubes and incubators, so they can be dissected with their parts sold to the medical community.

Ultimately, we should fight against abortion, child abuse, euthanasia and other such sins, but in the process we should not forget that the real battle needs to be waged against the underlying humanistic value system that determines acceptable and unacceptable behavior. We need to live by God's absolutes and teach them to the world around us. With our society crumbling upon the faulty foundation of evolutionary humanism, we should not be spending our time trying to patch the walls of our disintegrating culture's house. It is necessary that we concentrate our attention upon the rebuilding of the foundation that determines our society's values.

This is the proof that we are citizens of God's holy kingdom: both our attitudes and our actions will be honoring and glorifying to God. These two things combined will produce a Christian that serves the Lord by taking an active role in society.

Questions: Please indicate your answer with either True or False.

1. _____ Everyone who says, "Lord, Lord," shall enter into the kingdom. (Matt. 7:21)

2. _____ Everyone that prophesies in My name shall enter the kingdom. (Matt. 7:22-23)

3. _____ Everyone that does good works in my name shall enter the kingdom. (Matt. 7:22-23)

4. _____ Jesus will say unto them, "Depart from Me, ye that work iniquity." (Matt. 7:23)

5. _____ Whoever listens to Christ's sayings, is likened to a wise man. (Matt. 7:24)

6. _____ The wise man is the one who built his house upon the sand. (Matt. 7:24)

7. _____ The house that was built upon the rock did not fall. (Matt. 7:25)

8. _____ The foolish man is the one who built his house upon the rock. (Matt. 7:26)

9. _____ The people were astonished at the doctrine of Jesus. (Matt. 7:28)

10. _____ Jesus taught as One having authority and not as the scribes. (Matt. 7:29)

Thought Questions:

1. Explain why your life should be build upon a solid foundation. _____
   _____
   _____
   _____
   _____

2. Why is it necessary for society to base its values upon God's moral standards?
   _____
   _____
   _____

Lesson Review:

1. Why should you lay up your treasure in heaven? (Lesson #23) _____
   _____
   _____

2. Why is happiness something we should not strive or work toward? (Lesson #21) _____
   _____
   _____

3. What did Christ conquer when He rose from the dead? (Lesson #17)
   _____
   _____
   _____

The Substance of Faith
Lesson #25

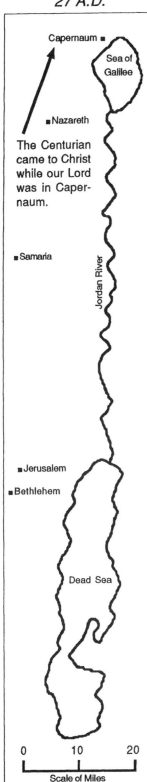

27 A.D.

Capernaum ■

Sea of Galilee

■ Nazareth

The Centurian came to Christ while our Lord was in Capernaum.

■ Samaria

Jordan River

■ Jerusalem

■ Bethlehem

Dead Sea

0   10   20

Scale of Miles

<u>Lesson Goal</u>: To understand what it means to have faith.

<u>Background Text</u>: Matthew 8:5-13; Luke 7:1-10

<u>Memory Verse</u>: Now faith is the substance of things hoped for, the evidence of things not seen. Hebrews 11:1

Every day we put our faith and trust in someone or something. This confidence can be exhibited in several different ways. We show faith in a chair by sitting in it. We show faith in a car by riding in it. We show faith in our parents by obeying them. We show faith in God by believing in Him. Every time we show faith, we are demonstrating that we believe that the person or object is going to do the thing it is supposed to do.

Our memory verse from Hebrews has an excellent definition of spiritual faith. "Now faith is the substance of things hoped for, the evidence of things not seen." As Christians, we believe in that which we cannot touch, hear, taste, smell, or see. We cannot see God, heaven or hell. We cannot touch the Holy Spirit. We are unable to smell eternal life or the angels. So how do we know if these things actually exist? We believe them on the basis of faith. Our trust lies in the truthfulness of God's Word. Like the centurion, our faith is not blind. It exists in the Lord Jesus Christ and in the power of His resurrection.

Why don't we believe in Allah, Buddha, or some other alleged deity? Because no one else has historically proven himself to be God. Only Jesus Christ, through fulfilled prophecy, miracles and the resurrection, proved that He was God's only begotten Son. To place our faith in anyone else would be ridiculous.

There are many people in the world today who have placed their faith in the wrong objects. Rather than believing in our Lord, they believe in themselves, money, jobs, good works, pagan idols, etc. Although they may be sincere in their belief, their faith is directed toward the wrong object. Someone once said that the road to Hell is paved with good

The Substance of Faith

intentions. Sincerity and faith have no power to save a person. Our Lord is very specific that we must believe in Him in order to be in good standing with God. Unless we personally believe in Christ and trust Him, our sincere faith, whatever it may be, is spiritually worthless.

Questions: Multiple Choice -- circle the correct answer for each question.

1. Where was Jesus when the centurion met Him? (Matt. 8:5)
    *Tarsus
    *Judaea
    *Capernaum
    *Samaria

2. What was wrong with the servant? (Matt. 8:6)
    *He was sick of the palsy.
    *He had leprosy.
    *He had an issue of blood.
    *He was blind.

3. What did the centurion want Jesus to do? (Matt. 8:8)
    *To come to his house
    *To have dinner with him
    *To cleanse him from his sins
    *To speak only the word

4. Over whom did the centurion have authority? (Matt. 8:9)
    *His slaves
    *His soldiers
    *Spirits
    *The guards of the palace

5. What did Jesus say the centurion had? (Matt. 8:10)
    *A nice personality
    *A great faith
    *A great love for his people
    *Perfection in this life

6. With whom shall they sit down? (Matt. 8:11)
    *Abraham, Moses and Joshua
    *Caleb, Isaiah and David
    *Abraham, Jacob and Isaac
    *Jacob, Isaac and Adam

7. When was the servant healed? (Matt. 8:13)
    *The next day
    *The same hour
    *A week later
    *Six days later

8. Just before Jesus went to Capernaum, what was He doing? (Luke 7:1)
    *He was eating with the publicans and sinners.
    *He was feeding 5000 people.
    *He was healing a blind man.
    *He was speaking to an audience of people.

9. Who did the centurion send to seek Jesus? (Luke 7:3)
    *The elders of the Jews
    *The Pharisees
    *The High Priest
    *The Sadducees

10. What did the centurion build for the nation? (Luke 7:5)
    *A synagogue
    *The temple
    *Many altars
    *A palace

Thought Questions:

1. What does it mean to you to have faith in God? _____
   _____
   _____
   _____
   _____

2. Since spiritual faith is in something that we cannot touch, hear, taste, smell or
   see, how do we know if God exists? _____
   _____
   _____
   _____

Lesson Review:

1. Explain the fact that the house built upon the rock was able to stand firm.
   (Lesson #24) _____
   _____
   _____

The Substance of Faith

2. How can a persecuted believer be happy? (Lesson #21) _____

_____

_____

3. How did the friends of the paralytic get him to Jesus? (Lesson #18) _____

_____

_____

<u>Supplemental Exercise</u>: Complete the crossword with the answers to the questions listed below.

1-A Opposite of east.

1-D Besides gnashing of teeth, this shall there be in the outer darkness. (Matt. 8:12)

2-A The centurion's servant was lying at home, sick with this. (Matt. 8:6)

3-D Jesus entered into this city. (Matt. 8:5)

4-D This individual came to Jesus, beseeching Him. (Matt. 8:5)

5-A Opposite of west.

6-A The son of Abraham.

7-D The grandfather of Jacob.

8-A The brother of John.

9-A The Son of God

10-D These individuals were under the authority of the Centurion. (Matt 8:9)

11-D The Centurion built many of this type of building. (Luke 7:5)

12-D "Go, and he goeth; and to _____, come, and he cometh." (Matt. 8:9)

13-A Christ did not find this kind of faith in Israel. (Matthew 8:10)

- 84 -

More Than Conquerors
Lesson #26

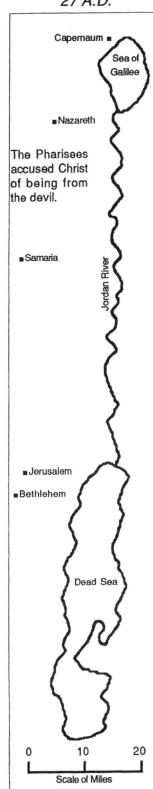

27 A.D.

Capernaum ■

Sea of Galilee

■Nazareth

The Pharisees accused Christ of being from the devil.

■Samaria

Jordan River

■Jerusalem

■Bethlehem

Dead Sea

0   10   20

Scale of Miles

Lesson Goal: To understand that through Christ we have victory over Satan and his demons.

Background Text: Matthew 12:22-37; Mark 3:22-30; Luke 11:14-23

Memory Verse: He that is not with me is against me; and he that gathereth not with me scattereth. Luke 11:23

A question arose among the people as our Lord was performing miracles: "How do we know that Christ is actually good, and not really a devil trying to trick us?" The Lord Jesus immediately responded to this insult by explaining how ridiculous the question was. If He were from Satan, why would He be casting demons from people? If this were true, He would be destroying the kingdom of Satan and thereby injuring Himself.

By commanding the demons to do as He willed, Christ demonstrated that He was more powerful than the devil. The evidence of this power climaxed when Christ died and rose from the dead. His crucifixion and resurrection completely destroyed Satan's kingdom. Christ conquered death and hell. "Death is swallowed up in victory. O death, where is thy sting? O grave, where is thy victory? The sting of death is sin; and the strength of sin is the law. But thanks be to God, which giveth us the victory through our Lord Jesus Christ." (I Corinthians 15:54b-57)

For believers, this power is demonstrated by our own victory over sin. Through the blood of Christ, Satan is a defeated enemy and unable to take charge of our lives. Romans 8:37 calls us "more than conquerors through Him that loved us." As a result, nothing (which would include Satan) can separate us from Christ Jesus. We cannot conquer this foe in our own strength, but we have this capability through the Lord Jesus Christ.

Satan is strong and we are not to take him for granted; however, we do not need to fear him. As believers, united together as the church, we have victory over Satan's

More Than Conquerors

kingdom. We can take confidence in the hope that no matter how much sin and wickedness there appears to be in the world, God's kingdom will reign triumphant. "And I say also unto thee, That thou art Peter, and upon this rock I will build my church; and the gates of hell shall not prevail against it." (Matthew 16:18)

<u>Questions:</u> Please indicate your answer with either True or False.

1. _____ When Jesus healed the man with the devil, his blindness and dumbness went away. (Matt. 12:22)

2. _____ When the people saw this, they called him the Son of Joseph. (Matt. 12:23)

3. _____ The Pharisees said that Jesus cast out devils by Beelzebub, the prince of the devils. (Matt. 12:24)

4. _____ Every city or house divided against itself is brought to ruin. (Matt. 12:25)

5. _____ If Satan casts out Satan, his kingdom is divided against itself. (Matt. 12:26)

6. _____ The scribes said that Jesus hath Beelzebub. (Mark 3:22)

7. _____ All sins and blasphemies shall be forgiven unto the sons of men. (Mark 3:28)

8. _____ One that blasphemes against the Holy Spirit will be forgiven and will be able to enter into eternal life. (Mark 3:29)

9. _____ Jesus knew the thoughts of those who were tempting Him. (Luke 11:17)

10. _____ Those who are against Jesus are for Him. (Luke 11:23)

Thought Questions:

1. How was Christ's death and resurrection able to destroy Satan's kingdom? ___
_____
_____
_____

2. What can you do to have victory over Satan's kingdom? _____
_____
_____
_____
_____

Lesson Review:

1. What three things help to prove that Christ Jesus was God's only **begotten**
Son? (Lesson #25) _____
_____
_____

2. Why shouldn't we worship Allah or Buddha? (Lesson #25) _____
_____
_____
_____

3. Why did the Jewish people strongly dislike the tax collectors? (Lesson #19) ___
_____
_____

Supplemental Exercise: Translate this Greek passage from John 1:14 into
English. The dictionary can be found in Appendix C.

και ο λογος σαρξ εγενετο και εσκηνωσεν εν ημιν

_____

και εθεασαμεθα την δοξαν αυτου

_____

δοξαν ως μονογενους παρα πατρος

_____

πληρης χαριτος και αληθειας

A Rocky Boat
Lesson #27

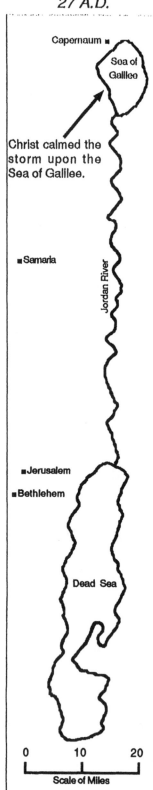

Capernaum ■

Sea of
Galilee

Christ calmed the
storm upon the
Sea of Galilee.

■Samaria

Jordan River

■Jerusalem

■Bethlehem

Dead Sea

0   10   20
Scale of Miles

<u>Lesson Goal</u>: To understand that we do not need to feel overwhelmed by problems.

<u>Background Text</u>: Matthew 8:18-27; Mark 4:35-41; Luke 8:22-25

<u>Memory Verse</u>: In God I will praise His Word, in God I have put my trust; I will not fear what flesh can do unto me. Psalms 56:4

What a surprise it must have been to the disciples when Christ calmed the storm! It would appear that they had already forgotten the miracles He had worked on land earlier in the day. Many of these disciples were fisherman and accustomed to storms on the sea, so it must have been a terrible storm to have caused them to be frightened by the wind and waves.

We are aboard a ship called life, traveling the sea of destiny. With us we have brought the necessary items that will provide for our basic needs and protect us through life's storms. Packed away in our suitcase we have our gifts, talents and abilities. We develop these to increase our spiritual, physical, intellectual, social and emotional well-being. As we mature, new opportunities, adventures and struggles will arise. Hopefully, we have prepared well enough that we can sail through them. Still, there will be times that, no matter how well we prepare, the storm will be too great for us.

During our journey, let us not neglect that which we have in our ship, the Lord Jesus Christ. Christ should not become a good luck charm that we pull out whenever we are in trouble. Christ should be the Captain and Navigator of our ship. When we rely upon Christ, not only will He protect us through the storms, but He will also guide our lives into the right channels.

Let us not so quickly forget God's purpose for our lives and become frightened when the storms arise. Though it may appear at times that our Lord is sleeping, He is ever watching and aware of what is happening to us. With this confidence, we need not fear the storms of life, but we can trust God to guide us through them.

Questions:

1. When Christ saw the multitudes, what order did He give His disciples? (Matt. 8:18) _____

_____

2. What did the scribe say to the Master? (Matt. 8:19) _____

_____

3. What do the foxes and birds have that the Son of Man does not have? (Matt. 8:20) _____

_____

4. What did one of His disciples want to do before he would go with Jesus? (Matt. 8:21) _____

_____

5. What did Jesus say to His disciple? (Matt. 8:22) _____

_____

6. What happened when Jesus and His disciples were in the boat? (Mark 4:37) __

_____

_____

7. What was Jesus doing when there arose a great storm? (Mark 4:38) _____

_____

8. What did the disciples say when they awakened Jesus? (Mark 4:38) _____

_____

9. What did Jesus say to the winds and the sea? (Mark 4:39) _____

_____

10. What did Jesus say the disciples lacked? (Luke 8:25) _____

Thought Questions:

1. What can we do to prepare ourselves for life's difficulties and struggles? _____

_____

_____

_____

_____

A Rocky Boat

2. What are some ways people use Christ like a good luck charm? _____

_____

_____

_____

_____

Lesson Review:

1. What completely destroyed Satan's kingdom? (Lesson #26) _____

_____

2. According to Hebrews 11:1, what is the definition of faith? (Lesson #25) _____

_____

3. How are you to appear to men when you fast? (Lesson #23) _____

_____

Mark Background

Author of Mark: Mark. He accompanied Paul and his uncle, Barnabas, on Paul's first missionary journey. About half-way through the journey, Mark left them and returned to Jerusalem (Acts 13:13). When Paul and Barnabas planned their second missionary journey, Barnabas wanted to bring Mark along again, but Paul was opposed. Paul and Barnabas split up, with Paul taking Silas and Barnabas taking Mark to Cyprus (Acts 15:36-41). Years later, Paul asked Timothy to bring Mark with him for the ministry (II Timothy 4:11). From this we can gather that whatever disagreement stood between Paul and Mark was now reconciled. Mark also had a close relationship with Peter (I Peter 5:13). Tradition teaches that Mark was Peter's convert and that he received most of the information for the writing of his gospel from Peter.

Date of Writing: Around A.D. 68

Purpose of Mark: To convince the Roman (Gentile) reader of the mission and deity of Christ Jesus.

Outline of Mark:

I.   The Introduction of the Servant (1:1-13)
    A.   His Forerunner (1:2-8)
    B.   His Baptism (1:9-11)
    C.   His Temptation (1:12-13)

II. The Ministry of the Servant (1:14-8:26)
    A.   Christ in Galilee (1:14-6:30)
        1.   Calls the Disciples (1:14-20)
        2.   Concern for the Sick and Lost (1:21-3:12)
        3.   Appoints the Twelve (3:13-21)
        4.   Accusations Against Christ (3:22-35)
        5.   Parables by the Seaside (4:1-34)
        6.   Calms the Storm (4:35-41)
        7.   Delivers the Maniac (5:1-20)
        8.   Raises the Daughter of Jairus (5:21-43)
    B.   Christ Withdraws from Galilee (Mark 6:1-8:26)
        1.   Opposition to the Righteous (6:1-29)
        2.   Feeds the 5000 (6:30-44)
        3.   Walks on the Water (6:45-52)
        4.   Teachings and Miracles (7:1-8:26)

III. Instruction of the Servant (8:27-10:52)
    A.   Jesus as Lord (8:27-38)
    B.   The Transfiguration (9:1-13)
    C.   The Necessity of Faith (9:14-29)
    D.   Teachings of Christ (9:30-10:45)
    E.   Healing of Bartimaeus (10:46-52)

IV   The Presentation and Rejections of the Servant (Mark 11-13)
    A.   The Entrance into Jerusalem (11:1-26)
    B.   Final Controversies with the Jewish Leaders (11:27-12:44)
    C.   The Olivet Discourse (Mark 13)

V.   The Passion of the Servant (Mark 14 & 15)
    A.   Treachery and Devotion (14:1-11)
    B.   The Passover (14:12-31)
    C.   Christ in Gethsemane (14:32-52)
    D.   Trial before Caiaphas (14:53-65)
    E.   Denial of Peter (14:66-72)
    F.   Trial before Pilate (15:1-15)
    G.   The Crucifixion (15:16-47)

VI.   The Resurrection of the Servant (Mark 16)
    A.   The Announcement of His Resurrection (16:1-8)
    B.   Appearances of Jesus (16:9-14)
    C.   The Great Commission (16:15-20)

Big Idea of Mark: The Gospel of Mark presents Christ as the servant of the Lord sent to accomplish a specific work for God. The habit of explaining Jewish terms and customs seems to indicate that the readers were not Jews nor did they have a good understanding of Jewish tradition. The Gospel of Mark is a book of details, not of words. It contains no long discourses and few parables, but is comprised mainly of the deeds and actions of Christ.

Mark is a book of action. Since the Roman mind was interested in power, Mark deliberately omitted the birth and childhood of Christ and quickly moved to His miracles. The typical Roman reader from that time period would have been impressed with the miracles performed by Christ. Mark's argument went from Christ's miracles to His deity and then to the greatest miracle and display of power: our Lord's death and resurrection. The Greek adverb "euthus" (straightway, immediately) is used forty-two times in Mark. This is more times than it appears in the rest of the New Testament combined. Christ is described as a man of action who got things done.

Mark emphasizes two major points in his Gospel. Chapters 1-10 cover the ministry and teaching of Christ. Chapters 11-16 concentrate upon the events surrounding the death and resurrection of our Lord. This book is built upon the concept of Christ the servant.

The Great Commission
Lesson #28

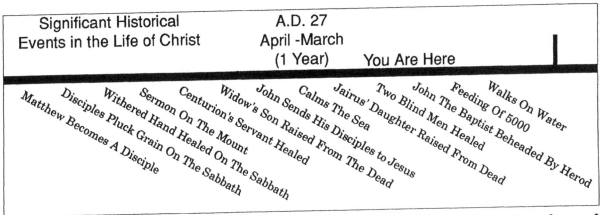

Matthew Becomes A Disciple

Disciples Pluck Grain On The Sabbath

Withered Hand Healed On The Sabbath

Sermon On The Mount

Centurion's Servant Healed

Widow's Son Raised From The Dead

John Sends His Disciples to Jesus

Calms The Sea

Jairus' Daughter Raised From Dead

Two Blind Men Healed

John The Baptist Beheaded By Herod

Feeding Of 5000

Walks On Water

<u>Lesson Goal</u>: To understand that our part in the Great Commission is to be and make disciples of Christ.

<u>Background Text</u>: Matthew 10:1-42; Mark 6:7-13; Luke 9:1-6

<u>Memory Verse</u>: Go ye therefore, and teach all nations, baptizing them in the name of the Father, and of the Son, and of the Holy Ghost: Teaching them to observe all things whatsoever I have commanded you. Matthew 28:19-20a

Have you ever asked yourself, "What is my mission in life? What purpose does my life have?" Did you even know that you have a mission? Well, you do. All Christians have a mission from God and it centers around the Great Commission.

The Great Commission was Christ's final instruction to His followers: to carry on His work after He ascended into heaven. He told them specifically to go, teach and baptize. This action was necessary in order to lead people to Christ. Notice that Christ did not tell His followers to get the people "saved," and then leave them to grow on their own spiritually. He told His disciples to teach them to observe all that He had commanded. Some evangelists miss this point. They have the tendency to be more concerned about the number of people that they supposedly save, than if those people truly commit their lives to Christ.

You shall receive power when the Holy Spirit comes on you.

The Great Commission

According to the Great Commission, our mission is to make disciples of all nations. Does this mean that we are to become missionaries and go to faraway countries? No, not necessarily, although God may lead some in that direction. What it means is that while we are going about our everyday activities, we are to make disciples of the people we know. This means that stronger, well-established believers, those who have a good understanding of God's Word, are to instruct and guide new believers and Christians that are spiritually immature.

Sometimes discipleship may take months. Other times it may take years. Consider that Christ even spent three years discipling His followers. In either case, discipleship involves a time commitment: one Christian, sharing his life with another, on a regular basis, in order to ensure that he is well established in the principles of God's Word.

This is our mission in life: to train believers so that they will become strong enough to disciple believers themselves. Now, you may not be an adult, or perhaps you have not been a Christian for very long. I would encourage you to seek out an older believer and ask him to help you grow in your spiritual walk. Still, even as a young Christian, you can talk with your friends and share with them what Christ means to you, teaching them the basic principles of God's Word that you have already learned.

Questions: Multiple choice -- circle the correct answer for each question.

1. What did Christ give the disciples power to do? (Matt. 10:1)
    *To cast out unclean spirits and to heal the sick
    *To give salvation to the lost
    *To walk on water
    *To turn water into wine

2. How many apostles did Jesus have? (Matt. 10:2)
    *Forty
    *Twelve
    *Ten
    *Seventy

3. Jesus sent His disciples as sheep in the midst of what? (Matt. 10:16)
    *Lions
    *Foxes
    *Doves
    *Wolves

4. What are we more valuable than? (Matt. 10:31)
    *Peacocks
    *Doves
    *Pigeons
    *Sparrows

5. What were the disciples to take with them? (Mark 6:8)
    *A staff
    *Bread
    *Money
    *A bag

6. What were the disciples to do when they were not welcomed in a house? (Mark 6:11)
    *Force their way in the house.
    *Curse the inhabitants of the house.
    *Kick off the dust under their feet as a testimony.
    *Stand outside and preach to them.

7. What did the disciples preach to the people? (Mark 6:12)
    *That they should repent.
    *Not to cheat on their tests.
    *To love thy neighbor as thyself.
    *Not to covet thy neighbor's belongings.

8. With what did they anoint the sick? (Mark 6:13)
    *Wine
    *Water
    *Vinegar
    *Oil

9. What were the disciples supposed to preach? (Luke 9:2)
    *Not to take the name of God in vain
    *The kingdom of God
    *To remember the Sabbath day
    *Not to bow down to any idols

10. How many coats were the disciples not to bring with them? (Luke 9:3)
    *No coats
    *One coat
    *Two coats
    *Three coats

Thought Questions:

1. What is your personal mission in life? What do you believe that God has called you to do? _____

_____

_____

_____

_____

_____

The Great Commission

2. Who is someone you know that can help you to grow in your spiritual walk? What could they do to help you? _____

_____

_____

_____

Lesson Review:

1. Why were the disciples scared when the storm arose? (Lesson #27) _____

_____

2. What question came up among the Pharisees when Christ performed miracles? (Lesson #26) _____

_____

3. Into what two categories can laws be divided? (Lesson #22) _____

_____

Supplemental Exercise: Solve the logic problem. (See page 17 for instructions.)

Each year the families would get together and meet in the center of their village for a special celebration. Among the many activities scheduled for this year's event was beekeeping. Isaiah persuaded a local artist to demonstrate a hobby that required a special skill. Those who attended were also fascinated, watching pots being shaped on a wheel. From the clues given below, can you match all five main events scheduled with the names of the demonstrators and his or her title or occupation?

1. The people were told to wear old clothes for anyone participating in Esther's activity. So were the people who participated in the activity led by the director.

2. The musician helped Nick's wife unload her spinning wheel.

3. The cook and Mary helped Anna set up her activity for children, "Paint with your feet!"

4. Only the potter showed the craft by which he earned his living; the others showed their hobbies.

5. The musician demonstrated glass blowing; he was engaged to the cook.

	Glass	Paint	Pottery	Spinning	BeeKeeping	Painter	Cook	Musician	Potter	Director
Anna										
Isaiah										
Esther										
Nick										
Mary										
Painter										
Cook										
Musician										
Potter										
Director										

Unit Test #2

Please indicate your answer with either True or False.

1. _____ The Jews said that Jesus had made Himself equal with God. (John 5:18)

2. _____ God did not give Jesus the authority to execute judgement. (John 5:27)

3. _____ Jesus said to Peter and Andrew, "Follow me, and I will make you fishers of men." (Matt. 4:19)

4. _____ Jesus said to the man who was sick with palsy that his sins were forgiven. (Matt. 9:2)

5. _____ The power of the Lord was present in Jesus to heal the sick. (Luke 5:17)

6. _____ The people who are well are the ones who need a physician. (Matt. 9:12)

7. _____ The poor in spirit will be comforted. (Matt. 5:3)

8. _____ Our righteousness must exceed the righteousness of the scribes and Pharisees. (Matt. 5:20)

9. _____ We are not to cast our diamonds before swine. (Matt. 7:6)

10. _____ Everyone who says, "Lord, Lord," shall enter into the kingdom. (Matt. 7:21)

11. _____ The wise man was the one who built his house upon the sand. (Matt. 7:24)

12. _____ The centurion sent the elders of the Jews to seek Jesus. (Luke 7:3)

13. _____ Every city or house divided against itself is brought to ruin. (Matt. 12:25)

14. _____ Jesus was preaching to the disciples when there arose a great storm. (Mark 4:37-38)

15. _____ The Lord Jesus had ten apostles. (Matt. 10:2)

A Miracle of Quantity
Lesson #29

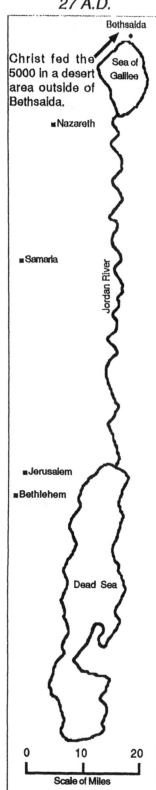

27 A.D.

Bethsaida

Sea of Galilee

Christ fed the 5000 in a desert area outside of Bethsaida.

■Nazareth

■Samaria

Jordan River

■Jerusalem

■Bethlehem

Dead Sea

0   10   20

Scale of Miles

Lesson Goal: To understand that God wants our availability, not simply our ability.

Background Text: Matthew 14:13-21; Mark 6:30-44; Luke 9:10-17; John 6:1-14

Memory Verse: Also I heard the voice of the Lord, saying, Whom shall I send, and who will go for us? Then said I, Here am I; send me. Isaiah 6:8

As we have been studying the life of our Lord, we have seen that the Gospel of John focuses upon seven of Christ's miracles. The miracle of the feeding of the five thousand is the fourth such event. This miracle had such a profound impact upon the Gospel writers that it is the only miracle, performed by Christ, mentioned in all four of the Gospels. Christ demonstrated, through this miracle that He was the Master of quantity. He could have fed five or 500,000 people. There was no limit to what God could do.

Let us spend a few moments looking at the life of the young lad who supplied Christ with the five loaves and two fish. There is a spiritual lesson that we can all learn from this miracle. One of the most important principles that I have discovered in my spiritual pilgrimage is that God does not need our ability; God desires our availability. He does not need the things that we can do; He desires us to be available for His use.

When Christ fed the five thousand, He did not have the disciples go into town to buy food. He did not cause bread to fall from the sky in the form of manna. He did not send someone out to a nearby deli to pick up some sandwiches. He used a simple boy with a simple lunch to demonstrate to the people the unlimited extent of His power. In this story, we have a young individual who said, "Here God, take whatever I have, no matter how seemingly insignificant, and use it for your glory."

We may think that what we know or what we can do is insignificant compared to the ability of others. However,

God would not call upon us if He did not want to use us. If God were a coach and life was a baseball game, there would be no bench-warmers on His team. Everyone would play in the game and no one would sit in the dugout. If anyone was on the sidelines or in the bleachers, it would be because they went there themselves and quit the game before it was over.

When God works His purpose in the world today, He does not just snap His fingers to make something happen. He uses His believers to accomplish His will. It is not so much that we have talents that God can use, though He does want us to develop our gifts and abilities. God wants us to be available to Him by our saying, "Here I am, use whatever I have for Your own will and purpose."

Questions:

1. When Jesus had heard that John the Baptist was dead, where did He go? (Matt. 14:13) _____

   _____

2. When Jesus saw the multitude, what type of feelings did He have towards the people? (Matt. 14:14) _____

3. What did the disciples say to Jesus concerning the people? (Matt. 14:15) _____

   _____

   _____

4. What did Jesus ask to be brought to Him? (Matt. 14:17-18) _____

   _____

5. Why was Jesus moved with compassion toward the multitude? (Mark 6:34) __

   _____

6. The people sat down in ranks of what? (Mark 6:40) _____

7. About how many men ate of this food? (Mark 6:44) _____

8. To what city did the desert place belong? (Luke 9:10) _____

9. What did Jesus do with the food the disciples gave Him? (Luke 9:16) _____

_____

10. How many baskets did the fragments of food fill? (John 6:13) _____

Thought Questions:

1. How can you make yourself more available to God? _____

_____

_____

_____

2. Why do you think God uses believers to accomplish His will, instead of simply doing it Himself?_____

_____

_____

_____

Lesson Review:

1. What were Christ's final instructions to His followers? (Lesson #28) _____

_____

_____

2. The people were living by a false assumption. What was it? (Lesson #22) ____

_____

_____

3. Who were the sons of Zebedee? (Lesson #16) _____

_____

Supplemental Exercise: Uncode the symbols to understand the message. The key is in Appendix B.

Miracle Over Natural Law
Lesson #30

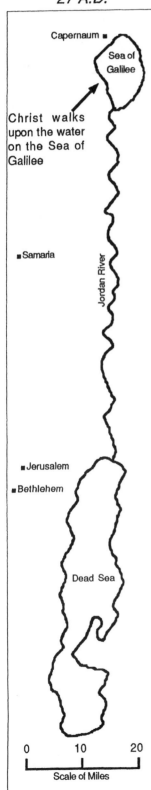

27 A.D.

Capernaum

Sea of Galilee

Christ walks upon the water on the Sea of Galilee

Samaria

Jordan River

Jerusalem

Bethlehem

Dead Sea

0   10   20

Scale of Miles

<u>Lesson Goal</u>: To understand that we must walk by faith, not by sight.

<u>Background Text</u>: Matthew 14:22-33; Mark 6:45-52; John 6:15-21

<u>Memory Verse</u>: For we walk by faith, not by sight. II Corinthians 5:7

In the Gospel of John, Christ's fifth miracle follows His fourth. Here John shows that Christ was the Master over natural law. It is humanly impossible to walk upon water, but our Lord could do it because He was God. When Peter came out to meet Christ upon the water, he was able to walk upon the surface because his faith in our Lord kept him from sinking. As soon as he began doubting, he went down.

In a previous lesson, we studied the biblical meaning of faith. We are going to take this concept one step further and discuss how we can walk by faith. As Christians, we daily commit our lives to the Lord. Part of this commitment is living a life of faith. In my childhood, my father would tow me in my sled behind the family snowmobile. I had no control over where he went or when he turned. I had to completely trust him to guide my sled around trees and past obstacles. I could always roll off the sled if I saw trouble approaching, but then I risked possible injury to myself. I had faith in my father that he would correctly guide and direct my sled.

My father is a very good man, and at no time did he ever abuse my trust in him. He was always careful to guide me around the dangerous situations. God is very much the same way. He leads and directs our lives, but we do not always know where He is going. Sometimes it may appear that our lives have no direction or purpose. As long as we do not jump off, but allow God to continue to pull us, He will guide us through the woods and into His paths of righteousness.

Miracle Over Natural Law

When Peter jumped out of the boat, he was fine as long as he trusted Christ and allowed Him to direct his steps. It was not until he took his eyes off of God that he was in trouble. For Christians, walking by faith means following God and obeying His Word. We will be safe, even in the midst of a storm, as long as we do not take our spiritual eyes off of our Lord Jesus.

Questions: Please indicate your answer with either True or False.

1. _____ After Jesus sent His disciples and the multitude away, He went onto a mountain to pray. (Matt. 14:23)

2. _____ When the disciples were in the ship, a great storm arose. (Matt. 14:24)

3. _____ Jesus went out to them in the sixth watch, walking on the water. (Matt. 14:25)

4. _____ The disciples were happy to see Christ walking to them on the water. (Matt. 14:26)

5. _____ Andrew asked the Lord if he could come out to Him on the water. (Matt. 14:28)

6. _____ When Peter took his eyes off Jesus to look at the wind, he began to sink. (Matt. 14:30)

7. _____ Jesus said to His disciples, "Be of good cheer: It is I; be not afraid." (Mark 6:50)

8. _____ When Jesus walked onto the ship, the winds ceased. (Mark 6:51)

9. _____ The disciples remembered the miracle of the loaves, so they were not afraid. (Mark 6:52)

10._____ The ship the disciples were in was headed towards Damascus. (John 6:17)

Thought Questions:

1. How does your faith guide you to Jesus during life's storms? _____

_____

_____

_____

_____

_____

2. Do you ever take your eyes off Christ and stop trusting Him? Explain your answer. _____

_____

_____

_____

_____

3. Give an example of a time you stepped out in faith and trusted Christ in an area that you could not control._____

_____

_____

_____

_____

_____

_____

Lesson Review:

1. Where did the disciples get the five loaves and two fish? (Lesson #29) _____

_____

_____

2. What was the fourth miracle recorded by John? (Lesson #29) _____

_____

_____

3. What did Christ come to send? (Lesson #28) _____

_____

_____

_____

Feeding the Four Thousand
Lesson #31

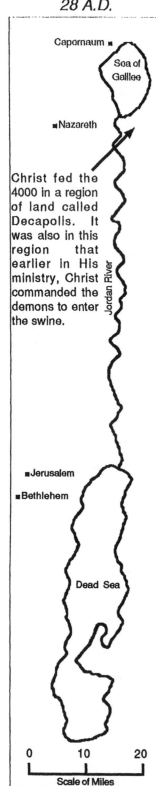

28 A.D.

Capornaum ■

Sea of Galilee

■Nazareth

Jordan River

Christ fed the 4000 in a region of land called Decapolis. It was also in this region that earlier in His ministry, Christ commanded the demons to enter the swine.

■Jerusalem

■Bethlehem

Dead Sea

0   10   20

Scale of Miles

Lesson Goal: To understand how not to neglect the power of God in our lives.

Background Text: Matthew 15:29-39; Mark 7:31-8:9

Memory Verse: But my God shall supply all your need according to His riches in glory by Christ Jesus. Philippians 4:19

When I was younger and did something wrong, my parents would sometimes scold me by saying, "How many times do I have to tell you to stop doing that?" Even now I find myself saying the same thing to my own children when they disobey. It is unfortunate, but so often we forget that which should be obvious to us. Like young children, we continually forget or even neglect the important lessons that God's Word tries to teach us.

The same thing happened to the disciples in verse 33 of Matthew 15. They had forgotten the miraculous power of Christ. Only a few days earlier, our Lord had fed the five thousand with five loaves and two fish. Now Christ reminds his disciples that He can work miracles of quantity by feeding four thousand with seven loaves and a few fish.

There hardly seems a day when we do not show the same ignorance and neglect of God's power in our lives. Because of our sinful nature, we oftentimes attempt to solve life's difficulties by our own strength or wit. Our neglect only leads to hardship and misery. We ought to be careful not to allow our minds to be drawn away from God's benefits toward us. He is capable of providing the same assistance to us in the future as He has in the past.

In II Peter 3:1-3, the apostle explains to his readers that he is writing to them to stir up their minds by way of reminder. Face it, we know that God is powerful and that He works through our lives. Still, we need to continually remind ourselves of this fact. Otherwise, we tend to lose sight of our service for the Lord. It is not so much that we doubt God; the disciples did not doubt that Christ could feed the multitude. It is rather that we forget that God is all-powerful and capable of handling our every need.

Questions:

1. Who came to Jesus while He was on the mountain? (Matt. 15:30) _____

   _____

2. What was the result of Christ's healing the people? (Matt. 15:31) _____

   _____

3. How long did the multitude stay with Him without anything to eat?
   (Matt. 15:32) _____

   _____

4. How many loaves and fishes did Jesus and His disciples have? (Matt. 15:34)

   _____

5. What did Jesus do with the food? (Matt. 15:36) _____

   _____

   _____

6. How many men did Jesus feed? (Matt. 15:38) _____

   _____

Feeding the Four Thousand

7. Where did Jesus and His disciples take their boat? (Matt. 15:39) _____

_____

8. What was wrong with the man who went to see Jesus? (Mark 7:32) _____

_____

9. What does Ephphatha mean? (Mark 7:34) _____

10. What did Jesus tell the man concerning this miracle? (Mark 7:36) _____

_____

Thought Questions:

1. List three things that God does of which you need to continually remind
   yourself. _____

_____

_____

_____

_____

_____

_____

2. Why do you think that people have the tendency to concentrate more upon the
   bad things that happen than upon the good things? _____

_____

_____

_____

_____

_____

_____

Lesson Review:

1. What was the only miracle which Christ performed that was mentioned in all
   four of the gospels? (Lesson #29) _____

_____

2. Describe the purpose of the Great Commission. (Lesson #28) _____

_____

3. In what hour was the servant healed? (Lesson #25) _____

_____

The Transfiguration
Lesson #32

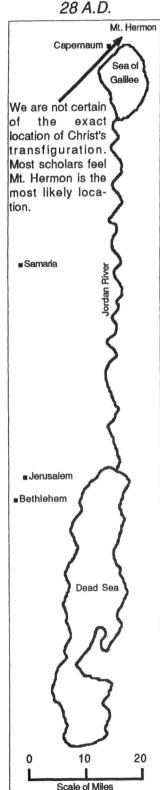

28 A.D.

Mt. Hermon

Capernaum

Sea of Galilee

We are not certain of the exact location of Christ's transfiguration. Most scholars feel Mt. Hermon is the most likely location.

Samaria

Jordan River

Jerusalem

Bethlehem

Dead Sea

0   10   20

Scale of Miles

Lesson Goal: To understand the sacrifice Christ made by taking the form of a man.

Background Text: Matthew 17:1-13; Mark 9:2-13; Luke 9:28-36

Memory Verse: But made Himself of no reputation, and took upon Him the form of a servant, and was made in the likeness of men: And being found in fashion as a man, He humbled Himself, and became obedient unto death, even the death of the cross. Philippians 2:7-8

It is difficult for us to imagine the sacrifices that Christ had to make by becoming a man. We generally think of Christ's sufferings as limited to the cross, including the scorn He received from the Roman and Jewish officials. We often neglect to remember that Christ had to leave His glory in heaven and take on a human body. This was necessary in order for Christ to become the perfect sacrifice for our sins.

Philippians 2:5-8 explains that Christ, being equal with God, took on the likeness of a man. Let us not forget that God is a spirit, and has no form or shape. When Christ came to earth, He humbled Himself by giving up the form of a spirit for the form of a man. Christ's sacrifice for us did not begin on the cross; it began when He made Himself to look like us.

Keep in mind that even when Christ had the body of a man, He did not stop being God. He was 100% God and 100% man, both at the same time. This was evident at His transfiguration where we see but a glimpse of His divine glory. Christ did not empty Himself of His divine nature or Godly attributes, but only the outward and visible manifestation of the Godhead. Christ may change forms, but He cannot cease to be God.

Someday, all those who believe in the Lord Jesus will be able to see Him in His complete glory. Just as Peter, James and John, we will be able to witness Him being more radiant than the sun. We will be able to fall down at His

The Transfiguration

This is my beloved Son

feet and give Him the worship and praise He deserves. Until then, we need to do what the voice from heaven commanded, "Hear Him." (Mark 9:7) Christ sacrificed His life in order that we may be reconciled with God. Let us listen to Him through His Word and Spirit in our hearts. In so doing we confess that Jesus is God and bring glory to the Father (Philippians 2:11).

<u>Questions</u>: Match the correct answer with the proper question.

1. _____ Who went with Jesus to the mountain? (Matt. 17:1)

2. _____ What happened as Christ was transfigured? (Matt. 17:2)

3. _____ Who appeared unto them? (Matt. 17:3)

4. _____ What did Peter want to build? (Matt. 17:4)

5. _____ What overshadowed them? (Matt. 17:5)

6. _____ What did the voice from heaven say? (Matt. 17:5)

7. _____ What did Jesus tell His disciples concerning His transfiguration? (Mark 9:9)

8. _____ Who do the scribes say must come first? (Mark 9:11)

9. _____ Why did Jesus take these disciples up to the mountain? (Luke 9:28)

10. _____ What were these disciples doing when the transfiguration was taking place? (Luke 9:32)

a. Moses and Elias

b. To pray

c. A bright cloud

d. Elias

e. Face shone like the sun

f. Sleeping

g. Peter, James and John

h. Not to tell anyone until He had risen from the dead

i. Three tabernacles

j. This is my beloved son in whom I am well pleased

Do all the good you can,
By all the means you can,
In all the ways you can,
In all the places you can,
At all the times you can,
To all the people you can,
As long as ever you can.

--John Wesley, His Rule

Thought Questions:

1. How can we listen to Christ Jesus? _____

_____

_____

_____

_____

2. Explain what it means when we say that Christ was 100% God and 100% man.

_____

_____

_____

_____

_____

Lesson Review:

1. How many baskets of food were left over when Christ fed the four thousand? (Lesson #31) _____

2. What was Christ's fifth miracle as recorded in the Gospel of John? (Lesson #30) _____

3. How did the Pharisees say that Christ cast out devils? (Lesson #26) _____

_____

Supplemental Exercise: There is a quotation concealed in this puzzle. The solution will be in one continuous line which goes through each of the words in the quotation. The words, which adjoin each other, read up, down, forwards, backwards and diagonally. Not all the letters will be used, and there are some extra words thrown in to confuse you. The quotation is taken from somewhere in the background text for this lesson. Find the quotation and discover the scripture reference from which it is taken and write it in this blank.

```
T I M E B E L L I G H T R
O H A P P Y I T I I V E R
D A E D E E F H E T V L E
O V T C H S T E S O N L V
U E A E T E H T L O T U E
N F R O M V T C F L A O N
B I O E O I A O M S E A X
E S A T S S T N A U M T C
L T U G T I L O N O C E E
I O S E A O T U M B E S T
E C I O V N E S I R E T P
```

The First Shall Be Last
Lesson #33

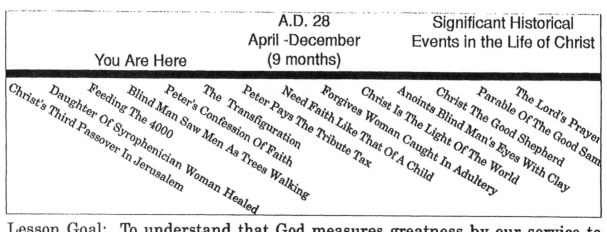

You Are Here	A.D. 28 April - December (9 months)	Significant Historical Events in the Life of Christ

Christ's Third Passover In Jerusalem
Daughter Of Syrophenician Woman Healed
Feeding The 4000
Blind Man Saw Men As Trees Walking
Peter's Confession Of Faith
The Transfiguration
Peter Pays The Tribute Tax
Need Faith Like That Of A Child
Forgives Woman Caught In Adultery
Christ Is The Light Of The World
Anoints Blind Man's Eyes With Clay
Christ The Good Shepherd
Parable Of The Good Sam
The Lord's Prayer

Lesson Goal: To understand that God measures greatness by our service to others.

Background Text: Matthew 18:1-6; Mark 9:33-41; Luke 9:46-48

Memory Verse: And whosoever of you will be the chiefest, shall be servant of all. Mark 10:44

It was no coincidence that the Gospel writers included this passage of Scripture after the transfiguration of our Lord. For three years the disciples had seen Christ heal the sick, walk on water, feed several thousand people and perform all types of miracles. Now Peter, James and John had just seen Him in His glory. It is little wonder that they began to be proud about their association with Christ and talk among themselves about being great.

At this point, the disciples may have misunderstood the purpose of Christ's ministry. Many people thought that Christ had come to overthrow the Roman empire, which held the Jewish people in subjection. The disciples may have imagined themselves to be generals and commanders in Christ's army. What they

failed to understand was that Christ had come to conquer sin, not Caesar.

Christ admonished the disciples by saying that they had to become as humble as children. Later, in Matthew 20:20-28, the mother of James and John asked Christ if

her sons could sit at His right and left hands in heaven. His response to her request was that if they wanted to be great in God's kingdom, they first had to be servants to everyone else. We find this same message taught throughout the Bible—that God wants His people to be humble servants. This does not merely imply being humble before God, but also humble before our fellow man.

This is contrary to what the world teaches us. Books are written and speeches are made on how, if we are to succeed in life, we need to be hard, selfish, greedy and cold. I do not recall hearing many people say that in order to get ahead in the world, you have to act like a humble child or servant.

Part of becoming a mature and strong Christian is developing spiritual qualities that are honoring to God. The fruit of the Spirit, listed in Galatians 5:22-23, are good examples of these qualities. Humility, then, is necessary in order to be a servant who pleases God. This means that we are to place a higher priority upon the needs of others than we place upon our own.

There are many things that one can do to help those who are in need or unable to care for themselves. Be a servant by visiting a hospital or nursing home. Mow the lawn or shovel the snow for people who are unable to do it for themselves. Even simple things like talking or being friendly to someone who is lonely are ways to be a servant. By being humble as a servant, we are not only being kind to others, but we are imitating the character of our Lord Jesus Christ.

Questions: Please indicate your answer with either True or False.

1. _____ The disciples asked Jesus, "Who is the least in the kingdom of heaven?" (Matt. 18:1)

2. _____ Jesus asked a little child to come to Him. (Matt. 18:2)

3. _____ We must be converted and become like a little child in order to enter the kingdom. (Matt. 18:3)

4. _____ If you humble yourself as a child, you will be like the greatest in heaven. (Matt. 18:4)

5. _____ Those who do not receive one such child will receive Jesus. (Matt. 18:5)

6. _____ If any man wants to be first, the same shall be last and master over all. (Mark 9:35)

The First Shall be Last

7. _____ John said to the Master that he saw a man casting out devils in Satan's name. (Mark 9:38)

8. _____ He that is against us is on our side. (Mark 9:40)

9. _____ Whoever shall give you a cup of water to drink in My name shall not lose his reward. (Mark 9:41)

10._____ He that is least among you shall be great. (Luke 9:48)

Thought Questions:

1. List three practical ways that you can demonstrate humility. _____

_____

_____

_____

_____

2. How can you be a servant of Christ to your family and friends? _____

_____

_____

_____

_____

Lesson Review:

1. How did Christ humble Himself? (Lesson #32) _____

_____

2. According to what shall God supply all your needs? (Lesson #31) _____

_____

_____

_____

_____

3. What consequences came as a result of David's sin? (Lesson #19)

_____

_____

_____

_____

Biblical Forgiveness
Lesson #34

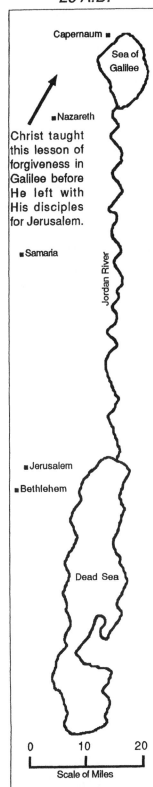

28 A.D.

Capernaum ■

Sea of Galilee

■ Nazareth

Christ taught this lesson of forgiveness in Galilee before He left with His disciples for Jerusalem.

■ Samaria

Jordan River

■ Jerusalem

■ Bethlehem

Dead Sea

0   10   20

Scale of Miles

Lesson Goal: To understand that along with forgiving sin, we may need to confront the sinner.

Background Text: Matthew 18:15-35

Memory Verse: For if ye forgive men their trespasses, your heavenly Father will also forgive you. Matthew 6:14

Many times throughout our lives, whether on purpose or by accident, people will hurt us or sin against us. Our simple response to these situations should be that of forgiveness. However, life is not always simple and neither are people's sins, so sometimes righteous steps need to be taken in order to correct the situation. If a fellow Christian has broken one of God's absolute standards, we are to forgive him, but we are also to go and confront him with his sin. The intention is not to condemn him, but to lead him to repentance through God's Word.

When someone wrongs us or sins against us, we are not to ignore it; nor are we to become bitter against the individual. We are biblically required to confront the person and attempt to make the situation right. If the person does not listen to us, then we are to take along one or two other people as witnesses to confront him again. What we are doing here is establishing a case against the person so that there is no doubt that he has actually wronged us.

It is strongly recommended that if a young person is confronting another individual, that he take his parents with him as witnesses. This will help to avoid confusion and give credibility to the young person's defense.

If the sinful person is not persuaded in front of the witnesses to repent, then the situation should be brought before the church. If the individual does not even listen to the church, the church is to cut him off from any of its activities and consider him a heathen. This may seem harsh, but this is necessary discipline in order to guide the sinner into repentance and back into fellowship with God and the church.

Biblical Forgiveness

Peter understood this teaching on confrontation and asked the Lord how often it was necessary to take these steps to forgive a habitual sinner. Christ said seventy times seven. Our Lord did not mean that we should forgive someone 490 times and then stop after that. He was implying that we should forgive that person every time.

By forgiving someone who has wronged us, we not only prevent ourselves from becoming bitter, but we also help the other person to reconcile his relationship with God. It is far easier to conveniently forget or overlook the unrighteous actions of another individual, than to confront him with the truth of God's Word.

Our role as Christians should not be taken lightly. It is a serious matter to accuse someone of sin, so be certain of your facts ahead of time. Confronting an unrepentant brother should only be done after careful prayer and consideration has been given to God's Word.

Questions:

1. What are you to do when your brother has offended you? (Matt. 18:15) _____

   _____

   _____

2. How many witnesses do you need to accuse someone of a fault? (Matt. 18:16)

   _____

3. Where is Christ when two or three are gathered together in His name? (Matt. 18:20) _____

   _____

4. Who is the one that came to Jesus and asked Him about forgiveness? (Matt. 18:21) _____

5. How many times did Jesus tell us to forgive a brother? (Matt. 18:22) _____

   _____

6. What is the kingdom of heaven like? (Matt. 18:23) _____

   _____

7. How much did the servant owe the king? (Matt. 18:24) _____

   _____

8. How much did the fellow servant owe the first servant? (Matt. 18:28) _____

_____

9. What did the first servant do to the fellow servant when he said he did not have the money? (Matt. 18:30) _____

_____

10. From where does forgiveness need to come? (Matt. 18:35) _____

_____

Thought Questions:

1. Is there anyone who has hurt you that you have not forgiven? What should your attitude be toward that person? _____

_____

_____

_____

_____

2. How can you develop an attitude of forgiveness with all people? _____

_____

_____

_____

_____

Lesson Review:

1. Christ admonished the disciples to be as humble as what? (Lesson #33) _____

_____

2. What did Christ give the disciples power to do? (Lesson #28) _____

_____

_____

3. Why are we supposed to lay up our treasure in heaven? (Lesson #23) _____

_____

_____

_____

_____

_____

_____

_____

Judge Not
Lesson #35

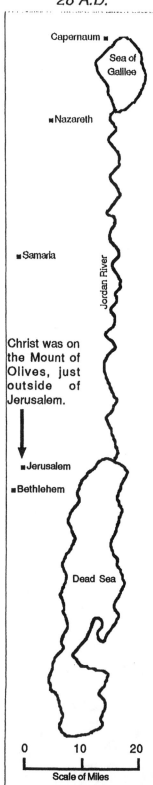

28 A.D.

Capernaum ■

Sea of Galilee

■ Nazareth

■ Samaria

Jordan River

Christ was on the Mount of Olives, just outside of Jerusalem.

■ Jerusalem

■ Bethlehem

Dead Sea

0   10   20

Scale of Miles

<u>Lesson Goal</u>: To understand the difference between condemning sin and unrighteously judging a brother.

<u>Background Text</u>: John 8:1-11

<u>Memory Verse</u>: So when they continued asking Him, He lifted up Himself, and said unto them, He that is without sin among you, let him first cast a stone at her. John 8:7

When Christ saved the woman from being stoned to death, He was not saying it was wrong to condemn sin. Our Lord hated wickedness and died to save us from the penalty of sin. Christ was attempting to teach that we should not be so quick to condemn in others the very sin that we commit ourselves.

In our previous lesson, we discussed forgiving and confronting a fellow Christian who had not repented from sin. That is completely different from unrighteous judging. Our Lord taught in Matthew 7:3-5, "And why beholdest thou the mote that is in thy brother's eye, but considerest not the beam that is in thine own eye? Or how wilt thou say to thy brother, let me pull out the mote out of thine eye; and, behold, a beam is in thine own eye? Thou hypocrite, first cast out the beam out of thine own eye; and then shalt thou see clearly to cast out the mote out of thy brother's eye." This means that we are not to be more concerned about other people's petty problems than we are about our own gross sins. Christ was condemning a problem that was not only existent back in the New Testament, but also today.

The Lord Jesus called people who said one thing and did another "hypocrites." He most commonly referred to the scribes and Pharisees as hypocrites. They were criticized by Christ because they told the people to live by the Law, even though they did not live by it themselves. So go ahead and confront sin, but make certain that you do not condemn in others the very sin that you practice yourself.

<u>Questions</u>: Multiple choice -- circle the correct answer for each question.

1. Jesus went to what mountain? (John 8:1)
   *Mount Hur
   *Mount of Olives
   *Mount Ararat
   *Mount Sinai

2. Where did Jesus go early in the morning? (John 8:2)
   *The temple
   *The synagogue
   *Jerusalem
   *Peter's home

3. Who did the scribes and Pharisees bring to Christ? (John 8:3)
   *A child
   *A man with leprosy
   *A woman taken in adultery
   *His mother

4. In the Law, who commanded that adulterers should be stoned? (John 8:5)
   *God
   *Moses
   *Deborah
   *David

5. Why did the Pharisees and scribes ask Jesus what He thought concerning this matter? (John 8:6)
   *They wanted to test His knowledge of the Law.
   *They wanted to take advantage of His kindness.
   *They wanted to please Jesus by asking His advice.
   *They wanted to tempt Him so that they might accuse Him.

6. What was Jesus doing while the Pharisees and scribes were talking? (John 8:6)
   *He was praying.
   *He was talking with the woman.
   *He was writing something on the ground.
   *He was enjoying His lunch.

7. What did Jesus say unto the Pharisees and scribes? (John 8:7)
   *He that is without sin...let him first cast a stone at her.
   *Judge not lest ye be judged.
   *Love your enemies as you would love yourself.
   *If you forgive others, God will forgive you.

8. What was the reaction of those that heard this saying? (John 8:9)
   *They forgave the woman.
   *They asked her over for dinner.
   *They were convicted by their own conscience.
   *They went through with their plans to stone her.

9. Who was left when the accusers went away? (John 8:10)
   *Jesus and His disciples
   *Jesus and the woman
   *The woman and Christ's disciples
   *Jesus and the Pharisees

10. What did Jesus say unto the woman? (John 8:11)
    *Neither do I condemn thee; go, and sin no more.
    *Do not commit adultery.
    *Forgive your accusers.
    *Do not judge those who have accused you.

Thought Questions:

1. Describe the difference between condemning sin and unrighteously judging a brother. _____
   _____
   _____
   _____

2. Why do you think that people have the tendency to condemn in others the very same sin that they commit themselves? _____
   _____
   _____
   _____
   _____

Lesson Review:

1. What are we biblically required to do if someone wrongs us or sins against us? (Lesson #34) _____
   _____
   _____

2. Blessed are the meek, for what shall they inherit? (Lesson #21) _____

3. What are the two major points that Mark emphasizes in his gospel? (Mark Background) _____
   _____

Miracle Over Misfortune
Lesson #36

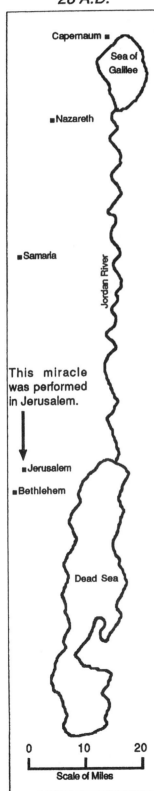

28 A.D.

Capernaum ■

Sea of Galilee

■Nazareth

■Samaria

Jordan River

This miracle was performed in Jerusalem.

■Jerusalem

■Bethlehem

Dead Sea

0   10   20

Scale of Miles

<u>Lesson Goal</u>: To understand that the righteous suffer in order to improve their character and thereby bring glory to God.

<u>Background Text</u>: John 9:1-41

<u>Memory Verse</u>: Search me, O God, and know my heart; try me, and know my thoughts; and see if there be any wicked way in me, and lead me in the way everlasting. Psalms 139:23-24

In this, the sixth miracle from John's gospel, Christ demonstrated that He was the Master over misfortune. It was unfortunate that this young man was blind. In an attempt to trick Christ, the Pharisees asked if any sin was responsible for the man's blindness. The Bible teaches that the underlining reason for all of man's problems is the sin nature; however, God will test His children and allow them to suffer for various reasons. Our Lord often permits a believer to be afflicted in order that his character may be purified.

This can be illustrated by the tempering of steel. In the metals industry, to temper the steel is to heat it to approximately 1200 degrees Fahrenheit and then allow it to slowly cool. By doing this, the steel actually becomes much harder and stronger. Through this process, the metal is tested by fire so as to improve its quality. In the same fashion, God will test the believer by bringing trials and struggles into his life in order to help him to stand strong against sin. The ultimate goal is for the believer to be obedient to the Lord.

No one knows what trials he will face, since God tests each Christian differently. For one person, the test may be the death of a loved one; for another person it may be a disease or sickness. We need to understand that through trials, God is not neglecting us. He is simply using difficult circumstances to improve the character of the believer. Just as a parent guides and directs the life of his child, God tests His believers so they will honor and glorify Him.

Miracle Over Misfortune

No matter how strong a Christian you are, suffering is still difficult. It would be so much easier if the believer could go through life without feeling any pain or heartache. A preacher once said, "When you find yourself in the middle of the sea of suffering without a boat or life jacket, it is too late to learn how to swim." God teaches us to swim by first getting us wet and then slowly taking us out into deeper water. This is necessary so that we will eventually be able to not only help ourselves, but also to swim out and save someone else who may be drowning in despair.

It is God's jealous desire that His people dedicate their lives to His service. God will then test and try the believer in order to make him stronger. This way the Christian will be more fully equipped to stand against sin and serve God.

Questions: Please indicate your answer with either True or False.

1. _____ When Jesus passed by, He saw a man who had been blind since birth. (John 9:1)

2. _____ His blindness was the result of sin in his life. (John 9:3)

3. _____ Jesus rubbed the eyes of the blind man with clay made with spittle. (John 9:6)

4. _____ The man washed his eyes in the pool of Hebron. (John 9:7)

5. _____ The Pharisees accused Jesus of not keeping the Sabbath. (John 9:16)

6. _____ The blind man called Jesus a prophet. (John 9:17)

7. _____ The Pharisees called the parents of the man to ask them whether he had been blind. (John 9:18)

8. _____ The Pharisees were disciples of Moses. (John 9:28)

9. _____ The Pharisees accused the man of unworthily teaching them. (John 9:34)

10. _____ The man never knew that Jesus was the Son of God. (John 9:35-38)

Thought Questions:

1. Why do you believe suffering and testing are important for the believer to experience? _____

_____

_____

_____

_____

2. What struggles has the Lord allowed into your life to test and improve your character? _____

_____

_____

_____

_____

3. What qualities have been improved in your life through God's testing? _____

_____

_____

_____

_____

Lesson Review:

1. How were the Pharisees hypocrites? (Lesson #35) _____

_____

2. What did Christ leave behind when He came to earth? (Lesson #32) _____

_____

_____

3. What was the name of the angel who appeared to Zacharias? (Lesson #2) ____

_____

The Good Shepherd
Lesson #37

28 A.D.

Capernaum

Sea of Galilee

Nazareth

Samaria

Jordan River

While in Jerusalem, Christ told several parables to teach the people about the Kingdom of Heaven.

Jerusalem

Bethlehem

Dead Sea

0   10   20

Scale of Miles

Lesson Goal: To understand why Christ calls Himself the Good Shepherd.

Background Text: John 10:1-21

Memory Verse: I am the good shepherd; the good shepherd giveth His life for the sheep. John 10:11

If you have ever had the opportunity to be around sheep, you may have discovered that they are very interesting animals. Compared to a cow or a horse, a sheep is quite ignorant. This is one of the reasons why sheep need a good shepherd. Without him, the sheep would wander off, get lost, and eventually get themselves eaten by a wild animal.

There is little wonder that Christ compares His followers to sheep. Without our Lord as the Shepherd we would lose our way in life and find ourselves in terrible trouble. It is only by the grace of God, and nothing that we do ourselves, that we believe in Christ and have life. Christ says that the sheep know the shepherd's voice and they follow it. As believers, we have the Bible as God's Word to instruct and guide us. It is our responsibility to listen for the Shepherd's voice by studying the Bible and then following its instructions.

The work of our Lord as the Good Shepherd has two purposes. As the "Good Shepherd," Christ not only provides life for His sheep, but He also gives His life for His sheep. Since He is the door through which all who enter will be saved, the sheep have to first go through Him before entering the fold. On the one hand, He provides protection, while on the other hand, He provides salvation. Both are necessary in order for His sheep to safely survive.

From this passage, we also see that Christ prophesied His own death. Our Lord illustrated this by explaining that a good shepherd lays down his life for his sheep. In the areas where the shepherd would take his sheep to graze, there were often wild animals which would attack the fold. A shepherd would risk his life against a lion or wolf in order to protect the lives of his sheep. The Lord Jesus not only risked His life, but He sacrificed it for His sheep in order for them to have eternal life.

Questions:

1. Who is the same as a thief or a robber? (John 10:1) _____

   _____

   _____

   _____

2. How does the shepherd call his sheep? (John 10:3) _____

   _____

   _____

   _____

3. How do the sheep know their shepherd? (John 10:4) _____

4. Who is the Door of the sheep? (John 10:7) _____

5. Whom did the sheep not hear? (John 10:8) _____

6. Why has the Shepherd come? (John 10:10) _____

   _____

7. Who does the Shepherd claim to know? (John 10:15) _____

8. Why does the Father love the Shepherd? (John 10:17) _____

   _____

9. Among whom was there a division because of these sayings of Christ? (John 10:19) _____

10. What did many people say Jesus had? (John 10:20) _____

Thought Questions:

1. What are some things from which the Lord protects us? _____

   _____

   _____

2. How is Jesus your personal Shepherd? _____

   _____

   _____

The Good Shepherd

Lesson Review:

1. How did Jesus heal the blind man at the synagogue? (Lesson #36) _____
   _____

2. What should we not be quick to do? (Lesson #35) _____
   _____
   _____

3. Who appeared to Jesus at His transfiguration? (Lesson #32) _____
   _____

Supplemental Exercise: Complete the crossword with the answers to the questions listed below.

1-A The name of the pool where the man was to wash. (John 9:7)

1-D If anyone confessed that he was the Christ, he would be put out from here. (John 9:22)

2-D "Why here is a _____ thing." (John 9:30)

3-A "_____ God the praise." (John 9:24)

4-A Christ anointed this part of the man's body. (John 9:6)

5-D The man asked the Jews if they wanted to be this. (John 9:27)

6-A Christ did this on the ground. (John 9:6)

7-D "Dost thou _____ on the Son of God?" (John 9:35)

8-A How the man got his sight. (John 9:11)

8-D "Therefore your sin _____." (John 9:41)

9-D Christ did this to the eyes of the blind man. (John 9:6)

10-A "I must _____ the works of Him that sent Me." (John 9:4)

10-D The man did this to the Lord. (John 9:38)

11-A "If any man be a worshipper of God, and _____ His will, him He heareth." (John 9:31)

12-D The Pharisees accused Christ of not doing this to the sabbath day. (John 9:16)

The Good Samaritan
Lesson #38

Significant Historical Events in the Life of Christ	A.D. 28 April -December (9 months)	You Are Here

Christ's Third Passover In Jerusalem
Daughter Of Syrophenician Woman Healed
Feeding The 4000
Blind Man Saw Men As Trees Walking
Peter's Confession Of Faith
The Transfiguration
Peter Pays The Tribute Tax
Need Faith Like That Of A Child
Forgives Woman Caught In Adultery
Christ Is The Light Of The World
Anoints Blind Man's Eyes With Clay
Christ The Good Shepherd
Parable Of The Good Sam
The Lord's Praye

<u>Lesson Goal</u>: To understand that we should be willing to go out of our way to show kindness to someone.

<u>Background Text</u>: Luke 10:25-37

<u>Memory Verse</u>: And be ye kind one to another, tenderhearted, forgiving one another, even as God for Christ's sake hath forgiven you. Ephesians 4:32

You cannot separate your relationship with God from your relationship with your fellow man. If you truly love God, you will love your neighbor. If you love your neighbor, you will show kindness to him. This is illustrated by our Lord in His parable of the good Samaritan.

As we discussed earlier, people may appear to be righteous, but unless they have a pure heart, and are committed to God, they are only pretending. The priest and Levite were pretending to be righteous. When they passed by the beaten man, they had no compassion for him. They were only concerned about getting as far away from this person as possible. They had no real love for God and therefore felt no desire to show love to their neighbor.

It was no accident that Christ made the hero of this story a Samaritan. A Samaritan was the least likely person to show compassion upon anyone coming out of Jerusalem. The Jews despised the Samaritans, and would generally go out of their way to avoid them. Nevertheless, the compassion of

The Good Samaritan

the Samaritan overcame any prejudices and was demonstrated to the injured man.

As believers, the test of our love for God is our love for our neighbor. However, we may have sinful prejudices or desires that keep us from demonstrating this love. It is necessary to confess these sins and reconcile ourselves to God. When we do this, we will have the freedom and compassion to open up our hearts to those who are in distress.

Questions:

1. With what question did the lawyer tempt Jesus? (Luke 10:25) _____
_____

2. What did the lawyer say was written in the Law? (Luke 10:26-27) _____
_____
_____
_____

3. What did the lawyer ask Jesus concerning his neighbor? (Luke 10:29) _____
_____
_____

4. What did the thieves do to the man who went down from Jerusalem? (Luke 10:30) _____
_____

5. Who was the first person who saw the man and passed by him? (Luke 10:31)
_____

6. Who was the second person who saw the man and passed by him? (Luke 10:32) _____

7. Who was the person that had compassion upon the man? (Luke 10:33) _____
_____

8. How did this man take care of the wounded man? (Luke 10:34) _____
_____
_____
_____

9. How much money did the man give to the host to care for the wounded man? (Luke 10:35) _____

10. Who was the neighbor to the man who fell among thieves? (Luke 10:36-37)
_____
_____

Thought Questions:

1. How can you be like the good Samaritan? _____
   _____
   _____
   _____

2. How can sinful prejudices keep you from loving your neighbor? _____
   _____
   _____
   _____
   _____

Lesson Review:

1. What two purposes does the work of our Lord as the Good Shepherd have?
   (Lesson #37) _____
   _____

2. Why do sheep generally need a shepherd? (Lesson 37) _____
   _____
   _____

3. What should you do when you confront someone with a sin they have
   committed and they do not listen to you? (Lesson #34) _____
   _____

Supplemental Exercise: Translate this Greek passage from John 14:6 into English. The dictionary can be found in Appendix C.

λεγει αυτω ο Ιησους

_____

Εγω ειμι η οδος και η αληθεια και η ζωη

_____

ουδεις ερχεται προς

_____

τον πατερα ει μη δι εμου

_____

The Rich Fool
Lesson #39

Capernaum ■

Sea of
Galilee

■ Nazareth

Jordan River

■ Samaria

This parable
was taught to
the people by
our Lord upon
the Mount of
Olives.

↓

■ Jerusalem

■ Bethlehem

Dead Sea

0   10   20

Scale of Miles

Lesson Goal: To understand the sin of covetousness.

Background Text: Luke 12:13-21

Memory Verse: And He said unto them, Take heed, and beware of covetousness; for a man's life consisteth not in the abundance of things which he possesseth. Luke 12:15

Oftentimes when our Lord was asked a question, He did not answer the issue directly, but rather went to the source of the problem. This is especially true in this passage where an individual complains to Christ about not receiving an inheritance from his brother. What was the motivation behind this man's request? It was not fairness or justice. It was covetousness. This man wanted something which he did not possess.

"Thou shalt not covet" is the last of the Ten Commandments. By coveting we can break all the other nine preceding commandments. Coveting can lead to many other sins that would eventually ruin us. Once as a child, I coveted a toy army tank that my best friend owned. It was really nothing special, a simple plastic toy, but I wanted it. I stole the tank and then lied to my parents to cover up the fact that I possessed it. My sins were eventually discovered and after being punished, I returned the tank.

Our Lord tries to explain to His listeners that it is unnecessary to covet. Why do we need to covet when God will provide for all of our needs? If we seek God's kingdom and righteousness, our Lord will bless and take care of us.

There is nothing sinful about being rich or possessing things. Some of the most spiritual individuals in the Bible were also the richest. Abraham, David, Solomon, Job and Hezekiah were all very wealthy and had very close relationships with God. It is when we love money and seek after material possessions more than we seek after God and His kingdom that we sin.

Christ advises us that the solution to coveting is not to

worry about life, but to store up our treasure in heaven. In other words, the good works we do on the earth will be rewarded in heaven. By serving God and loving our neighbor, we place a higher priority upon God's kingdom than we do upon our own interests. Missionary Jim Elliott once wrote, "He is no fool to give what he cannot keep to gain what he cannot lose."

Questions: Multiple choice -- circle the correct answer for each question.

1. What did one of the company ask Jesus to do? (Luke 12:13)
    *To heal his brother
    *To tell his brother that he has no right to any of the inheritance
    *To pray for him
    *To tell his brother to divide the inheritance

2. What did the Master say unto the man? (Luke 12:14)
    *I will do what you ask of Me.
    *I will not do what you ask of Me.
    *Go tell him yourself.
    *Who made Me a judge or divider over you?

3. Of what did Jesus tell the listeners to beware? (Luke 12:15)
    *Lying
    *Hatred
    *Covetousness
    *Drunkenness

4. What did the rich man have? (Luke 12:16)
    *Many friends
    *Ground that brought forth plentifully good crops
    *A large house
    *Many cattle

5. What was his concern about his fruits? (Luke 12:17)
    *There was too much room for them.
    *He did not know how to divide them among his family.
    *There was not enough room to store his fruits.
    *He did not want to give his fruits to the Pharisees.

6. What was the rich man's answer to the problem concerning the fruits? (Luke 12:18)
    *He would tear down his barns and build greater ones.
    *He would use his friend's barns.
    *He never found an answer.
    *He would give all the fruits away to the Pharisees.

The Rich Fool

7. What did the rich man say to his soul? (Luke 12:19)
   *Keep working hard
   *Take thine ease, eat, drink and be merry
   *I am a greedy man.
   *Go and tell others that the Messiah has come

8. What did God call the rich man? (Luke 12:20)
   *A fool
   *A Godly man
   *An adulterer
   *A man worthy of praise

9. What was required of the rich man? (Luke 12:20)
   *He would need to make restitution.
   *His fruits
   *His soul
   *He would have to give up everything he owned.

10. To whom are we to lay up treasures? (Luke 12:21)
    *God
    *Satan
    *Ourselves
    *The church

Thought Questions:

1. Have you ever coveted anything, and if so, how did you overcome it? _____

   _____

   _____

   _____

   _____

2. What is something that you can do to store up your treasure in heaven? _____

   _____

   _____

Lesson Review:

1. If you love God, to whom will you also show love? (Lesson #38) _____

   _____

2. Who were the two men who walked past the injured man? (Lesson #38) _____

   _____

3. What do the foxes and birds have that the Son of Man does not have?
   (Lesson #27) _____

Lost and Found
Lesson #40

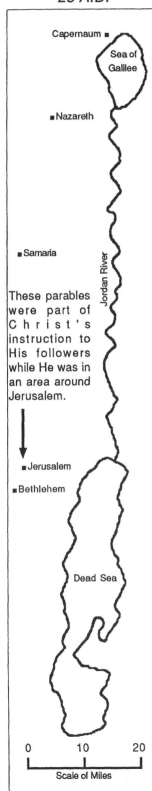

28 A.D.

Capernaum ■

Sea of Galilee

■ Nazareth

■ Samaria

Jordan River

These parables were part of Christ's instruction to His followers while He was in an area around Jerusalem.

■ Jerusalem

■ Bethlehem

Dead Sea

0   10   20

Scale of Miles

Lesson Goal: To understand what happens to believers when they fall away from the Lord.

Background Text: Luke 15:1-32

Memory Verse: Likewise, I say unto you, there is joy in the presence of the angels of God over one sinner that repenteth. Luke 15:10

The three parables taught by our Lord in Luke 15 are all related and should be studied together as one unit. The common element, in each of these parables, is that something which the owner possessed was lost, then later found, causing the owner to rejoice. Each of these stories teaches the principle that God rejoices when a sinner repents of wickedness and turns to follow the Savior. Whether the individual is a believer or a non-believer, these parables speak directly of Christ's love toward the individual out of fellowship with God.

When a Christian walks away from God by sinning and not trusting Him, our Lord considers that person lost. This does not mean that the person is no longer saved. The Bible makes it very clear that once a person is a true believer, salvation cannot be lost or taken away from him (Ephesians 1:13-14). Rather, when a Christian is lost, He is living in a state of sin and out of fellowship with God.

Notice throughout these parables that Christ does not abandon the sinner or forget about Him. The love of Christ extends to this individual to bring him to repentance and into fellowship with God. It is a sad state when a believer falls into sin, as in the case of the prodigal son, but there is a time of great rejoicing when he repents and comes back to God.

As believers, we do not want to fall into sin. Paul says, "What shall we say then? Shall we continue in sin that grace may abound? God forbid. How shall we, that are dead to sin, live any longer therein?" (Romans 6:1-2) However, if we do fall into sin for a time, we have hope and confidence that God will receive us back and rejoice to have us trust Him once again.

There are some individuals who feel that because of some past sin, Christ will not love or accept them. This is simply not true. Christ rejoices more for the return of the lost individual than for all the others who did not go astray. Does this mean that Christ loves the sinner more than the believer? No, it means that Christ is happy when a sinner repents and is brought into fellowship with God. I John 1:9 says, "If we confess our sins, He is faithful and just to forgive us our sins, and to cleanse us from all unrighteousness."

If you know of anyone who has sinned, but then has repented and sought the Lord's forgiveness, be kind to that person and have fellowship with him. Oftentimes, church members and fellow Christians treat a repentant Christian too harshly. We all have a tendency to judge too much and not forgive enough. Accept a repentant believer as a friend and help him to become a stronger Christian.

<u>Questions</u>: Please indicate your answer with either True or False.

1. _____ The Pharisees and scribes murmured saying that Jesus was not the Son of God. (Luke 15:2)

2. _____ When a man has found his lost sheep, he calls his friends and neighbors to rejoice with him. (Luke 15:6)

3. _____ When one sinner repents there is joy in heaven. (Luke 15:7)

4. _____ When a woman loses a piece of silver, she will do nothing to find it. (Luke 15:8)

5. _____ The older son wanted the portion of goods that belonged to him. (Luke 15:12)

6. _____ The younger son went into a far country where he wasted his substance on riotous living. (Luke 15:13)

7. _____ War began to spread throughout this land. (Luke 15:14)

8. _____ The younger son decided to go home and repent before his father. (Luke 15:18)

9. _____ The father received him and put the best robe on him. (Luke 15:22)

10. _____ The older son was so happy that his brother had returned that he joined the party. (Luke 15:28)

Thought Questions:

1. Why do you think Christ rejoices when a person repents from sin? _____

_____

_____

_____

_____

2. Why should we be willing to accept a person who has repented from sin? _____

_____

_____

_____

Lesson Review:

1. How can coveting lead you to break other commandments? (Lesson #39) _____

_____

_____

_____

2. What are the fruits of the Spirit? (Lesson #33) _____

_____

_____

_____

3. Jesus sends His disciples as sheep in the midst of what? (Lesson #28) _____

_____

The Raising of Lazarus
Lesson #41

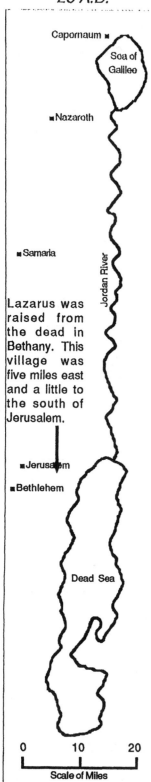

28 A.D.

Capernaum ■

Sea of Galilee

■ Nazareth

■ Samaria

Jordan River

Lazarus was raised from the dead in Bethany. This village was five miles east and a little to the south of Jerusalem.

■ Jerusalem

■ Bethlehem

Dead Sea

0   10   20

Scale of Miles

<u>Lesson Goal</u>: To understand that we need to wait upon the Lord and have patience in His will.

<u>Background Text</u>: John 11:1-57

<u>Memory Verse</u>: But they that wait upon the Lord shall renew their strength; they shall mount up with wings as eagles; they shall run, and not be weary; and they shall walk, and not faint. Isaiah 40:31

The seventh and final miracle that John recorded to support Christ's claim to deity was the most significant. Through it Christ demonstrated that He had the power to bring back life from the dead. Christ's miracles gave credibility to His ministry and His control over functions that man was unable to direct. Quality, space, time, quantity, natural law, misfortune and death — these all define humanity's world. Daily existence is a struggle against the limitations they set. Christ's superiority over them was proof positive of His deity and omnipotence.

When Mary and Martha informed Jesus that Lazarus was sick, no doubt they imagined that our Lord would heal him. They were followers of Christ and were familiar with the miracles He had performed. They had learned that Christ had the power to heal those who were ill; so, when they told Jesus about Lazarus' sickness, they expected that he would be healed.

It came as quite a shock to these women when their brother Lazarus died. They did not understand why Christ had allowed this death to happen. Since Christ had healed so many people throughout His ministry, why could He not heal someone who was His close friend? These women had lost sight of the fact that God does not always do things according to our wishes, but according to His will.

We are often like Mary and Martha when we bring a prayer or request before the Lord. If we do not see immediate results, we become discouraged and wonder if God actually heard us. The Bible admonishes us to wait upon the Lord and have patience in His will (Psalms 37:7-9). He may not answer our prayers the way we plan, but He will answer them according to His plan. We can have hope and confidence that God, in His perfect wisdom, knows better what we need and want, than we know ourselves. Garrison

Keillor has written, "Some [fortune] lies in not getting what you thought you wanted but getting what you have, which once you have it you may be [wise] enough to see is what you would have wanted had you known." Think about it.

Questions:

1. Why did the disciples not want Jesus to go to Judea? (John 11:7-8) _____
_____

2. When Jesus said that Lazarus was sleeping, of what was He speaking? (John 11:13) _____
_____

3. How many days was Lazarus in the grave before Jesus came? (John 11:17) ___
_____

4. Who were Lazarus' sisters? (John 11:19) _____

5. Who stayed at home when the news came that Jesus was coming? (John 11:20) _____
_____

6. What did the Jews think when Mary went out to meet Jesus? (John 11:31) ___
_____

7. What did Jesus do when He saw Mary weeping? (John 11:33-35) _____
_____

8. What did Jesus say to Lazarus? (John 11:43) _____
_____

9. Where did some of the Jews go to report this miracle? (John 11:46) _____
_____

10. To what city did Jesus and His disciples go when they found out that the Jews wanted to kill Jesus? (John 11:53-54) _____
_____

The Raising of Lazarus

<u>Thought Questions</u>:

1. Why do you think it seems to take so long for God to answer some of our prayers? _____

_____

_____

_____

_____

2. Based upon what you have learned about the Lord Jesus, what kind of comfort would you give someone who has just lost a loved one through death? _____

_____

_____

_____

_____

<u>Lesson Review</u>:

1. Why did the **prodigal son come back home**? (Lesson #40) _____

_____

_____

2. How many sheep did the shepherd leave to find the one which was lost? (Lesson #40) _____

3. Why does Jesus use the example of sheep in His parable of the Good Shepherd? (Lesson #37) _____

_____

<u>Supplemental Exercise</u>: Complete the puzzle and find the hidden phrase.

Then they took away the [1] from the place where the dead was laid. And Jesus [2] up his eyes, and said, "Father, I thank thee that thou hast heard me. And I knew that thou hearest me always; but, because of the people who stand by I said it, that they may [3] that thou hast [4] me." And when he thus had spoken, he cried with a loud voice, "Lazarus, come forth." And he that was dead came forth, bound [8] and [7] with [6]; and his face was bound about with a [5]. Jesus saith unto them, "Loose him, and let him go." (John 11:41-44)

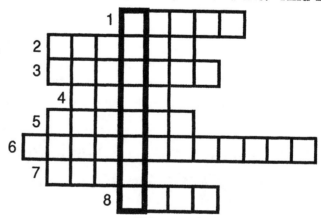

The Ten Lepers
Lesson #42

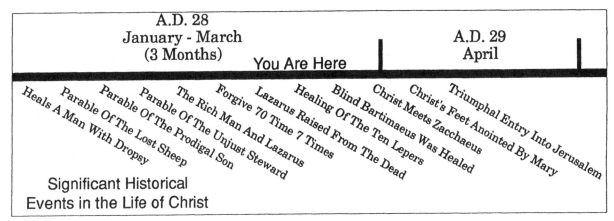

A.D. 28 January - March (3 Months)	A.D. 29 April

You Are Here

Heals A Man With Dropsy
Parable Of The Lost Sheep
Parable Of The Prodigal Son
Parable Of The Unjust Steward
The Rich Man And Lazarus
Forgive 70 Time 7 Times
Lazarus Raised From The Dead
Healing Of The Ten Lepers
Blind Bartimaeus Was Healed
Christ Meets Zacchaeus
Christ's Feet Anointed By Mary
Triumphal Entry Into Jerusalem

Significant Historical
Events in the Life of Christ

Lesson Goal: To understand the principle of gratitude.

Background Text: Luke 17:11-19

Memory Verse: In every thing give thanks; for this is the will of God in Christ Jesus concerning you. I Thessalonians 5:18

If you are like most Christians, you probably thank God for your food before you eat your dinner and say your prayers before you go to sleep. Yet, how often do you thank God for your parents, your health and your home? Most people say "thank you" when someone hands them a gift; but how often do you go up to someone and thank them for what they mean to you? Each of you have had people that have helped you at one point or another in your lives. They may have been friends who have listened to you, teachers who have positively directed you, or parents who have loved you. No doubt you are grateful for these people, but do you show this gratitude as you should?

Gratitude can be shown in many different ways. The most meaningful ways of saying "thank you" can also be the simplest. You do not have to rent an airplane to write a message in the sky in order to tell someone that you appreciate them. All it takes is a kind gesture or a warm comment. Unfortunately, we become so busy and self-centered that we neglect, or even forget, the kindness shown to us by other people.

Take this opportunity to do something nice for someone who has been kind to you. Send a card or stop by to say "hello." Congratulate a person for something, or tell them that you appreciate all the kindness they have shown to you in the past. Do not end up being one of the nine lepers who did not say "Thank you" to our Lord. Instead, make it a habit to be someone who shows appreciation by being thankful and gracious to those that are around you.

The Ten Lepers

Questions: Please indicate your answer with either True or False.

1. _____ When Jesus went to Judea, He passed through Samaria and Jerusalem. (Luke 17:11)

2. _____ Jesus met ten lepers in a certain village. (Luke 17:12)

3. _____ They asked Jesus to have mercy on them. (Luke 17:13)

4. _____ Jesus told them to go show themselves unto the priests. (Luke 17:14)

5. _____ When they went their way they were cleansed. (Luke 17:14)

6. _____ When two of the lepers saw that they were healed, they went back to thank God. (Luke 17:15)

7. _____ The leper who thanked Christ was a Jew. (Luke 17:16)

8. _____ The leper shook Christ's hand and thanked Him for the miracle. (Luke 17:16)

9. _____ Jesus asked, "Where are the other eight men?" (Luke 17:17)

10. _____ Jesus said, "Thy faith hath made thee whole." (Luke 17:19)

Thought Questions:

1. What is something that you can do today to specifically show your gratitude to your parents? _____

_____

_____

_____

2. What is something that you can do today to specifically show your gratitude to God? _____

_____

_____

_____

_____

Lesson Review:

1. Who comforted Martha and Mary after Lazarus' death? (Lesson #41) _____

   _____

2. What was the common element in the three parables from Luke 15? (Lesson #40) _____

   _____

   _____

3. What are the six major points in the outline of the Gospel of Mark? (Mark Background)_____

   _____

   _____

   _____

Supplemental Exercise: Unscramble the seven words listed below. Take the letters that are circled and rearrange them to solve the missing phrase. Clue: the missing phrase is from this lesson's story.

MASAARI

ERSSIPT

LAEDEH

NSEAELCD

LSRAMEEUJ

YOLRG

OCSVIE

— — — — — — — , — — — — — — — — — — — — — .

Luke Background

<u>Author of Luke</u>: Luke. He also wrote the book of Acts to a new convert by the name of Theophilus. Luke was a companion and fellow worker with Paul on his missionary journeys (Philemon 24). Paul calls Luke the "beloved physican" (Colossians 4:14), which seems to indicate that Luke was a doctor. Luke was probably the only writer of the Gospels who was a Gentile.

<u>Date of Writing</u>: Around A.D. 60

<u>Purpose of Luke</u>: The purpose is directed to Theophilus in (Luke 1:4), "That thou mightest know the certainty of those things, wherein thou hast been instructed."

<u>Outline of Luke</u>:

I.   Introduction (1:1-4)

II.   The Announcement of the Son of Man (1:5-2:52)
        A.   The Announcement to Zacharias (1:5-25)
        B.   The Annunciation to Mary (1:26-56)
        C.   The Birth of John (1:57-80)
        D.   The Birth of Jesus (2:1-20)
        E.   The Presentation in the Temple (2:21-40)
        F.   The Visit to Jerusalem (2:41-52)

III.   The Appearance of the Son of Man (3:1-4:15)
        A.   The Introduction of John the Baptist (3:1-20)
        B.   The Baptism of Jesus (3:21-22)
        C.   The Genealogy of Jesus (3:23-38)
        D.   The Temptation of Jesus (4:1-13)
        E.   The Entrance into Galilee (4:14-15)

IV.   The Ministry of the Son of Man (4:16-9:50)
        A.   The Definition of His Ministry (4:16-44)
        B.   The Proof of His Power (5:1-6:11)
        C.   The Choice of His Apostles (6:12-19)
        D.   A Digest of His Teaching (6:20-49)
        E.   A Cross Section of His Ministry (7:1-9:17)
        F.   The Climax of His Ministry (9:18-50)

V.   The Journey of the Son of Man (9:51-18:30)
        A.   The Perspective of the Cross (9:51-62)
        B.   The Ministry of the Seventy (10:1-24)
        C.   Popular Teaching (10:25-13:21)

D.   The Beginning of Public Debate (13:22-16:31)
E.   Instruction of the Disciples (17:1-18:30)

VI.   The Suffering of the Son of Man (18:31-23:56)
     A.   The Progress to Jerusalem (18:31-19:27)
     B.   The Entry into Jerusalem (19:28-44)
     C.   The Teaching in Jerusalem (19:45-21:4)
     D.   The Olivet Discourse (21:5-38)
     E.   The Last Supper (22:1-38)
     F.   The Betrayal (22:39-53)
     G.   The Arrest and Trial (22:54-23:25)
     H.   The Crucifixion (23:26-49)
     I.   The Burial (23:50-56)

VII.   The Resurrection of the Son of Man (Luke 24)
     A.   The Empty Tomb (24:1-12)
     B.   The Road to Emmaus (24:13-35)
     C.   The Appearance to the Disciples (24:36-43)
     D.   The Great Commission (24:44-49)
     E.   The Ascension (24:50-53)

Big Idea of Luke: Luke wrote specifically to Theophilus and in general to the Greeks. He emphasized the perfect humanity of Christ. Christ is presented as the Son of man, the human-divine person.

Some of the famous liturgical hymns of the church are based upon the five unique songs or poems of praise contained in Luke's opening chapters.

Song of Elizabeth	1:39-45
Mary's Response	1:46-55
Song of Zacharias	1:67-79
Angel's Rejoicing	2:13-14
Praise of Simeon	2:28-32

Luke stresses people and elevates the role of women. He refers to women forty-three times. Christ's birth is viewed from Mary's perspective; whereas, Matthew viewed it from Joseph's perspective.

Luke is the most complete account of the life of Jesus. Almost 60% of this Gospel is unique to the other Gospels. It was designed to be a full presentation of the career of the Savior from His birth to His ascension, and was part of a larger work including the book of Acts, which carried the history into the missionary activity of the early church.

Unit Test #3

Multiple choice -- circle the correct answer for each question.

1. Why was Jesus moved with compassion toward the multitude? (Mark 6:34)
    *They were as sheep not having a shepherd
    *They were sick and hungry
    *They did not know who He was
    *Christ was full of love

2. What happened when Jesus walked onto the ship? (Mark 6:51)
    *The disciples jumped into the water
    *It went to shore
    *The winds ceased
    *He fell asleep

3. What does Ephphatha mean? (Mark 7:34)
    *Have a good day
    *Come quickly Lord Jesus
    *Blessed
    *Be opened

4. What did Peter want to build? (Matt. 17:4)
    *Chariots
    *Tabernacles
    *Temples
    *A house on the solid rock

5. What are you to do when a brother has offended you? (Matt. 18:15)
    *Turn the other cheek
    *Give him lots of money
    *Punch him in the nose
    *Go and tell him his fault

6. Who did the scribes and Pharisees bring to Christ? (John 8:3)
    *A child
    *A man with leprosy
    *A woman taken in adultery
    *His mother

7. What did Jesus say unto the woman? (John 8:11)
    *Neither do I condemn thee; go, and sin no more.
    *Do not commit adultery.
    *Forgive your accusers.
    *Do not judge those who have accused you.

8. With what did Jesus rub the eyes of the man? (John 9:6)
    *Clay of the spittle
    *Water
    *The leaf of a palm tree
    *The crutch of a lame man

9. How do the sheep know their shepherd? (John 10:4)
    *They know his smell
    *They know his voice
    *They know his touch
    *They do not know the shepherd, they are ignorant

10. Of what did Jesus tell the listeners to beware? (Luke 12:15)
    *Lying
    *Hatred
    *Covetousness
    *Drunkenness

11. What did God call the rich man? (Luke 12:20)
    *A fool
    *A Godly man
    *An adulterer
    *A man worthy of praise

12. What happens when one sinner repents? (Luke 15:7)
    *The angels sing praises
    *He earns a stone in his crown
    *He builds his house upon the rock
    *There is joy in heaven

13. How many days was Lazarus in the grave before Jesus came? (John 11:17)
    *Two Days
    *Four Days
    *Six Days
    *Twelve Days

14. What did Jesus do when He saw Mary weeping? (John 11:33-35)
    *He questioned her lack of faith
    *He comforted her
    *He wept
    *He asked her not to cry

15. What did the leper do when he saw he was healed? (Luke 17:15-16)
    *He went his way and forgot about Christ
    *He glorified God with a loud voice
    *He told everyone in town about Christ
    *He danced up and down in the street

The Gift of Worship
Lesson #43

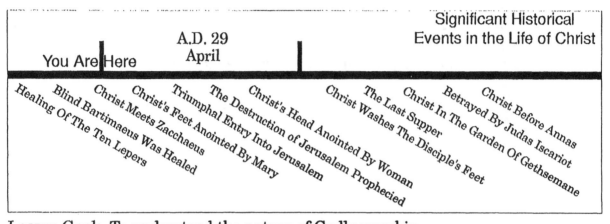

Significant Historical
Events in the Life of Christ

A.D. 29
April

You Are Here

Healing Of The Ten Lepers
Blind Bartimaeus Was Healed
Christ Meets Zacchaeus
Christ's Feet Anointed By Mary
Triumphal Entry Into Jerusalem
The Destruction of Jerusalem Prophecied
Christ's Head Anointed By Woman
Christ Washes The Disciple's Feet
The Last Supper
Christ In The Garden Of Gethsemane
Betrayed By Judas Iscariot
Christ Before Annas

Lesson Goal: To understand the nature of Godly worship.

Background Text: Matthew 26:6-13; Mark 14:3-9; John 12:1-11

Memory Verse: Give unto the Lord the glory due unto His name: bring an offering, and come before Him: worship the Lord in the beauty of holiness. I Chronicles 16:29

Worship can be simply defined as the demonstration of our love toward someone. When a husband and wife love each other, they demonstrate a form of worship. They may bring gifts to one another, talk and spend time together, cuddle and hold each other. These physical displays of affection are intended to show the other person that they are loved.

When we love God, we can worship Him in three basic ways. First, we can bring gifts to Him. Although we cannot present our gifts to God directly, we can show our appreciation to Him by giving of our time and resources, being kind to our neighbors and helping those who are in need. Matthew 25:40 says that by giving to the least of the brethren, we give to God. This is a demonstration of our love to others, through which God is worshipped and honored.

Next, we can worship God by learning about Him and studying His Word. When we love and care for another person, we want to get to know them better, understand who they are, what they feel, and spend time with them. We can get to know God by reading, memorizing and meditating on the Bible. Through God's Word, we can understand Who our Savior and Lord actually is, what He likes and dislikes, and how He wants us to live. When we spend time in God's Word, His Spirit speaks to our hearts and we have communion and fellowship with Him. There have been many times as I have read the Bible and prayed that I was spiritually drawn closer to God. Through this, I understand Him better and therefore grow to love Him more.

Finally, we can worship God by singing and giving praise to His holy name. We have several examples of this outward display of worship written in the Psalms. David and the writers of the Psalms sing praises to God by explaining His attributes (Psalm 139) and by reviewing His goodness to the people throughout history (Psalm 78). By worshipping God in this fashion, we remind ourselves of who God is and reaffirm our knowledge of His love and watchful care over us.

Worship is more than simply going to church, praying or singing songs. It is the complete display of our love toward God in every area of life. By giving to others, studying God's Word, and praising Him, we worship our Lord and present Him with honor, glory and praise. These ingredients solidify our relationship with God and guide us into a closer and stronger relationship with our Lord Jesus Christ.

Questions:

1. In whose house was Jesus while He was in Bethany? (Matt. 26:6) _____

_____

2. What did the woman pour on Christ's head? (Matt. 26:7) _____

_____

3. When did she do this? (Matt. 26:7) _____

4. Why did the disciples get angry with the woman? (Mark 14:4) _____

_____

5. What did some suggest should have been done with the ointment? (Mark 14:5)

_____

_____

6. For what reason did Jesus say the woman did this? (Mark 14:8) _____

_____

7. Who was the one that suggested a different use for the ointment? (John 12:4-5)

_____

8. Why did this man give his suggestion? (John 12:6) _____

_____

9. Who did the people come to see? (John 12:9) _____

10. Who were the people that consulted to put Lazarus to death? (John 12:10) __

_____

The Gift of Worship

Thought Questions:

1. What are some ways that you can worship Christ? _____

    _____

    _____

    _____

    _____

2. Why do you think that worship is a necessary part of the believer's spiritual life? _____

    _____

    _____

    _____

    _____

Lesson Review:

1. How did the one leper show his gratitude to Jesus for healing him? (Lesson #42) _____

    _____

2. Why did the nobleman seek Jesus? (Lesson #14) _____

    _____

3. How did Jesus feel after He fasted forty days? (Lesson #10) _____

    _____

Supplemental Exercise: Uncode the symbols to understand the message. The key is in Appendix B.

_____

_____

_____

_____

_____

The Return of the King
Lesson #44

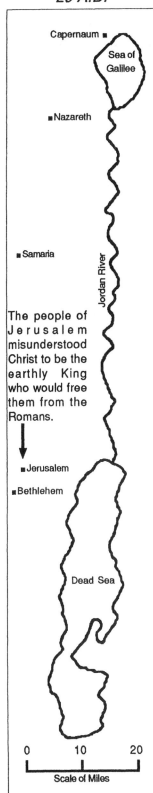

29 A.D.

Capernaum ■

Sea of Galilee

■ Nazareth

■ Samaria

Jordan River

The people of Jerusalem misunderstood Christ to be the earthly King who would free them from the Romans.

■ Jerusalem

■ Bethlehem

Dead Sea

0   10   20

Scale of Miles

Lesson Goal: To understand that the Jews misunderstood and later rejected the message of Christ.

Background Text: Matthew 21:1-11; Mark 11:1-11; Luke 19:29-44; John 12:12-19

Memory Verse: O Jerusalem, Jerusalem, which killest the prophets, and stonest them that are sent unto thee; how often would I have gathered thy children together, as a hen doth gather her brood under her wings, and ye would not! Luke 13:34

The scene was one of excitement and joy. Thousands lined the streets as Christ rode past upon His donkey. "Hosanna!" the people cried, "Blessed is the new King of Israel!" At last, they thought, a ruler to free us from the Romans and make Israel a great nation once again. They were wrong in both of these assumptions.

When Christ came to Jerusalem, He did not come as a military leader. His purpose was not to overthrow the Roman government. Christ came to Jerusalem to die and to release men from the bondage of sin. Within six days of Christ's triumphal entry into the city, the people wanted Him dead. What had once been songs of praise became shouts of condemnation. They imagined that they had been tricked by this One who called himself King.

Looking upon Jerusalem, our Lord wept. He loved the city and its people and wanted to gather them to Him as a chicken does her chicks. However, the Jews were unwilling. They rejected Christ and His message. They did not accept the fact that He was their Messiah.

Even today many Orthodox Jews are still waiting for the Messiah to come to earth. Since they do not consider Christ the Son of God, they misunderstand the prophecies of the Old Testament and completely reject the message of the New Testament. They still seek their atonement by means of the Laws of Moses found in the first five books of the Old Testament.

The Return of the King

Although the Jews in Jerusalem were disappointed when they found out that Christ was not going to be their earthly King, those who believed upon Him as their Savior were glad that He was their heavenly King. Christ died for something more important than nations, rulers or politics. He died so we could have life and eternal fellowship with God the Father.

Questions:

1. When they drew nigh unto _____ and were come to Bethphage, unto the _____, then sent Jesus two of His disciples. (Matt. 21:1)

2. Jesus told them to go into a _____ and there they would find an _____ and a _____. (Matt. 21:2)

3. If any man were to say anything, the disciples were to say "_____ _____." (Matt. 21:3)

4. All this was done which was spoken by the _____. (Matt. 21:4)

5. They brought the _____ to Jesus and they cast their _____ upon him. (Mark 11:7)

6. And many spread their _____ in the way while others cut down _____ off the _____. (Mark 11:8)

7. The multitude of disciples began to _____ and _____ God for all the mighty _____ that they had seen. (Luke 19:37)

8. And some of the _____ from among the _____ said unto him, "_____, rebuke thy disciples." (Luke 19:39)

9. The people took _____ of the _____ trees and cried, _____! Blessed is the _____ of _____, that cometh in the name of the _____. (John 12:13)

10. The people that were with Him when He called _____ from the _____ bare record. (John 12:17)

Thought Questions:

1. What does Christ's death mean to you? _____

_____

_____

_____

_____

2. What can you do to show your friends that Christ loves them? _____

_____

_____

_____

Lesson Review:

1. Explain three different ways that we can worship God. (Lesson #43) _____

_____

_____

2. What did the shepherd do when one of his sheep was missing? (Lesson #40) __

_____

3. Explain why the priest and Levite were unrighteous. (Lesson #38) _____

_____

Supplemental Exercise: Complete the puzzle and find the hidden phrase.

And a very great multitude spread their [3] in the way; others cut [2] branches from the trees, and strewed them in the way. And the multitudes that went before, and that [5], [6] saying, "Hosanna to the Son of David! Blessed is he that cometh in the name of the [4]! [1] in the highest!" And when he was come into [7], all the city was [8], saying, "who is this?" And the [10] said, "This is Jesus, the prophet of Nazareth of [9]." (Matthew 21:8-11)

Landscaping 101
Lesson #45

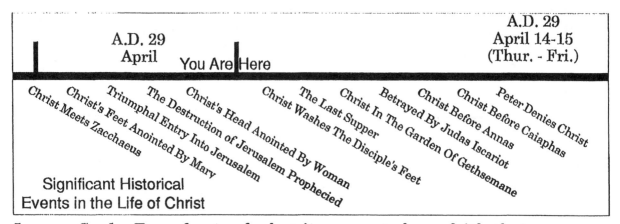

A.D. 29
April

You Are Here

A.D. 29
April 14-15
(Thur. - Fri.)

Christ Meets Zacchaeus
Christ's Feet Anointed By Mary
Triumphal Entry Into Jerusalem
The Destruction of Jerusalem Prophecied
Christ's Head Anointed By Woman
Christ Washes The Disciple's Feet
The Last Supper
Christ In The Garden Of Gethsemane
Betrayed By Judas Iscariot
Christ Before Annas
Christ Before Caiaphas
Peter Denies Christ

Significant Historical
Events in the Life of Christ

Lesson Goal: To understand what it means to have faith that can move mountains.

Background Text: Matthew 21:20-22; Mark 11:20-26

Memory Verse: Therefore I say unto you, what things soever ye desire, when ye pray, believe that ye receive them, and ye shall have them. Mark 11:24

Most colleges categorize their classes numerically by the hundreds. An entry level freshman class would be 101; whereas, an advanced level senior class would be 401. Imagine taking a college class in landscaping with this description: "Rearrange your backyard; remove unsightly waste deposit dumps; improve your office view -- all this can be learned through 'moving mountains by faith' in this course: Landscaping 101." It sounds silly, but what did Christ mean when he told His disciples that if they had faith, they could move mountains?

Faith can be applied to our lives in a number of different ways. It does not end at the moment of salvation. Faith continues to grow and develop in the believer's life as he places his trust and obedience in the Lord. In this context, to have faith in God means to expect and be fully assured of obtaining, from Him, whatever we need.

Christ does not give a blank check to the carnal wishes of man, that they should desire and attain anything for their pleasure. The blessings of God come as result of abiding in His Word and living in obedience to His will. Our Lord guides and directs the desires of His believers through the Holy Spirit within them. Therefore, God's blessings do not apply to His followers unless they keep themselves within the guidance of His will.

To believers, Christ says to ask for whatever we desire and it will be done for us.

Matthew 7:7 promises, "Ask, and it shall be given you; seek, and ye shall find; knock, and it shall be opened unto you." When our desires are those of God's, He will provide us with the things necessary to fulfill His plan and purpose.

We have this great assurance that we will not lack anything necessary to accomplish God's will upon this earth. If we have a seemingly insurmountable obstacle in our life (i.e. a spiritual mountain), we have but to ask God to remove it, have faith that it will be done, and it will be. As disciples of Christ, our Lord has promised to provide for our every need. Ephesians 3:20 explains that Christ is able to do exceeding abundantly above all that we ask or think, according to the power that works within us.

Questions: Please indicate your answer with either True or False.

1. _____ The disciples marvelled at how soon the fig tree was withered. (Matt. 21:20)

2. _____ If you have enough faith you can say to this mountain, "Be thou removed, and cast into the sea," and it shall be done. (Matt. 21:21)

3. _____ Whatsoever ye ask in prayer believing, ye shall not receive. (Matt. 21:22)

4. _____ In the afternoon they passed by the withered fig tree. (Mark 11:20)

5. _____ Paul called to remembrance what the Master had said concerning the fig tree. (Mark 11:21)

6. _____ Jesus told them to have faith in God. (Mark 11:22)

7. _____ If you have doubt in your heart, you can still move mountains. (Mark 11:23)

8. _____ If you have faith and believe that those things will come to pass, then they will come to pass. (Mark 11:23)

9. _____ You must believe that God will grant those things for which you are praying. (Mark 11:24)

10. _____ You should forgive others because our Father will forgive us. (Mark 11:25)

Landscaping 101

<u>Thought Questions</u>:

1. Does having faith mean that a person can have whatever he wants? Explain your answer. _____

_____

_____

_____

_____

2. Why do some Christians suffer if God supplies our every need? _____

_____

_____

_____

<u>Lesson Review</u>:

1. Why did the people's praise turn into shouts of condemnation? (Lesson #44) __

_____

2. How does studying the Bible help to strengthen our relationship with God? (Lesson #43) _____

_____

_____

3. What was the purpose of the Gospel of Luke? (Luke Background) _____

_____

<u>Supplemental Exercise</u>: Find and circle the words listed in the word search puzzle. Words may be forward, backward, horizontal, vertical or diagonal.

Mountain	Peter	Sun
Shine	Brother	Jesus
Raiment	Glistering	John
James	White	Light
Moses	Elijah	Lord
Cloud	Awake	Son
Vision	Suffer	Snow
Baptist	Beloved	Sleep
Decease	Master	Voice
Feared	Jerusalem	Face
Overshadowed		
Transfigured		
Tabernacles		

```
S N A M O U N T A I N Q Z O G K O
T Y F G V U E N I H S E S O M S M
U M T N E M I A R I B E L O V E D
E X R I R K E R L O R D M I L L X
E P E R S E A P E T E R T A J C A
C T F E H Z S W J R N T S G J A P
I H F T A F D I A H H U I B L N H
O G U S D U A E O B R O T H E R R
V I S I O N F J C E E W P T W E T
E L D L W X U E J E C O A H V B W
K S C G E N O S V C A N B M Q A B
L X Z A D E R U G I F S N A R T I
N C O J W D P S M A S T E R N U Y
```

The Widow's Offering
Lesson #46

29 A.D.

Capernaum ■

Sea of Galilee

■Nazareth

■Samaria

Jordan River

The temple treasury was located in Jerusalem.

■Jerusalem

■Bethlehem

Dead Sea

0   10   20

Scale of Miles

<u>Lesson Goal</u>: To understand that by giving to God, we demonstrate our love and commitment to Him.

<u>Background Text</u>: Mark 12:41-44; Luke 21:1-4

<u>Memory Verse</u>: Commit thy way unto the Lord; trust also in Him; and He shall bring it to pass. Psalms 37:5

When Christ told the disciples the story of the widow's offering, He was not merely speaking of money. Remember, this event took place only a few days before Christ's crucifixion and He knew the destiny that awaited Him. Christ was saying that when we give our lives to God, we are to give everything. We are not to hold back a small portion for ourselves.

Look back to the story of the rich young ruler (Matthew 19:16-30). He had kept all of the commandments and wanted to follow Christ but he was unwilling to give up his possessions. It wasn't that Christ wanted or needed his

The Widow's Offering

money. Christ wanted the young man to give Him the highest priority in his life.

In the Sermon on the Mount, our Lord said that we cannot serve two masters (Matthew 6:24). We will either hate the one and love the other or we will hold the one and despise the other. We cannot serve both God and material possessions. A wise man once said that God not only owns the cattle on a thousand hills, but he owns the hills as well. Our Lord is not advocating that we live a life of poverty. Money, in and of itself, is not evil. Only when we make it more important to us than God's kingdom, does it become wrong.

How do you know if God holds the highest priority in your life? Ask yourself if there is anything that you would be unwilling to sacrifice for the sake of Christ. Would you be willing to lose all your friends and family members, or give up the things which you possess and cherish the most? If you can honestly say that you are willing to sacrifice everything for your relationship with God, then He holds the highest priority in your life.

Questions: Multiple choice -- circle the correct answer for each question.

1. Where was Jesus sitting? (Mark 12:41)
    *Next to the synagogue
    *Over against the treasury
    *Next to the temple
    *Over against the temple

2. What was Jesus observing? (Mark 12:41)
    *How the tax collectors were getting their money
    *How the people listened to the priest's teachings
    *How the Pharisees were giving their money to Caesar
    *How the people cast their money into the treasury

3. Who were the people that cast much money into the treasury? (Mark 12:41)
    *The rich
    *Christ's disciples
    *The tax collectors
    *The Priests

4. How much money did the poor widow give? (Mark 12:42)
    *Three farthing
    *Two mites
    *One pence
    *More than one year's income

5. How much does two mites equal? (Mark 12:42)
    *One pence
    *One cubit
    *Three farthing
    *One farthing

6. To whom was Jesus talking about the woman? (Mark 12:43)
   *The Sadducees
   *The disciples
   *The Pharisees
   *The priests

7. What did Jesus say concerning the woman? (Mark 12:43)
   *This woman is greedy.
   *This woman has stolen from the treasury.
   *This woman gave more than everyone else.
   *This woman did not give all she had.

8. Of what did the others give their money? (Mark 12:44)
   *Of their abundance
   *Of their entire living
   *Of their entire inheritance
   *Of their entire family

9. Of what did the woman give her money? (Mark 12:44)
   *Of her abundance
   *Of her want
   *Of her entire inheritance
   *Of her entire family

10. Where did the Pharisees cast their abundance? (Luke 21:4)
    *In the temple
    *Unto the offering of God
    *Into the offering basket
    *On the street

Thought Questions:

1. Why do you think that some people find it difficult to give God the highest priority in their lives? _____

   _____

   _____

   _____

   _____

2. How can we use money and material wealth in our service for the Lord? _____

   _____

   _____

   _____

   _____

   _____

The Widow's Offering

<u>Lesson Review</u>:

1. Through whom does the Lord guide and direct our lives? (Lesson #45) _____

   _____

2. Into what two categories can laws be divided? (Lesson #22) _____

   _____

3. Where is Jacob's well? (Lesson #13) _____

   _____

<u>Supplemental Exercise</u>: See how many of the 178 names listed in the four Gospels you can find in this word search. Words may be forward, backward, horizontal, vertical or diagonal. Note: different publishers of the King James Version of the Bible may use different spellings for some of the names. The complete listing of the names may be found in the Teacher's Guide to this book.

```
C A T X A P L H A L E S U H T E M R P T H O M A S U E H C C A Z
B A R T H O L O M E W L R Z N E U E I W I B A D A N I M M A I E
E P E A T U L D C E B E I E A F R T L Z L A S A C V L X M I N L
E U R S R E E A R C H E L A U S U A I C E R D H H E A O Q A A O
L E J S A T I D M T U A R S K C E A H Y H T R A I J S N H P T T
Z R O R M R N E A E D Z E E Y I G H P E D I H T M E A S N H A E
E V S S E A A F M G C J Z R T G M A R R T M L A S H H M R A S S
B I E T L M D G A E O H E I A E I N O B B A R R I O Q U E S O I
U A S Q I R A M U N S N I N A S P L C X E E L S N R Z H H S M J
B A H N S O Y T A S I I L S E H A B N H S U R I P A U A S M Q O
M J H C H R B H T U T N E U D E O G S O A S Q M P M E N A N J H
T O I R A C S I S A D U J E I R J U O N M P A O G S A N N A M N
J N M M O R W A H T T O S H V O E T N D M A D N D S U E A M I T
H A I D A M L P B S S H A P A D K A E A A O D U J E A I A P R H
A S A S M L A N C I V X I L D B S H T W T Y I O L N Y H T A O E
I S A I A H C S A R J R Y A E U I T V A T B E N M B A P R N J B
M N J J S A D H O H A A H S S V H T M S A H P O E L C H S O O A
E Z A O B I C E U C T T H W U E I A I D T N Y M A I E E O J E P
R P H S S K R G H S A T A U W M R M F H H R N L D C R I N R L T
E E D E B E Z E R U B B A B E L E M O L A S E A O U X C R A I I
J L I P M Z L F B S I S R M E O H D N M U E O S G D L H S B J S
B E D H J E S S E E A G O T N T O N O R L G U L F E C M E O A T
O G Y E F H L G I J T I N E E K B D A C D R Z I O O W R A M H G
C O M F O R T E R K H R N S F H O Z H H I E H P N M I E O A H M
A A U H H L M S A N A M A A N O A H U A T N H E O U O D T Z T A
J R S J A J E B A A R I N A S L M I J U D A H J S J R N E O E H
N P D U I L E U B I H C N M L Y E E R T S O N C A I N A N R B T
A H L D E L A R N C D O A O E G L G I A H B A H E O R X B L A O
B A R A B B A S A A J O J E C H O N I A H E L U R P A E U B S J
M X Z S R H B R U T H Q R G M O S B R O S C B Z F H H L N O I A
N A T H A N A E L L P P N E K S H E E A N M E A A E V A M K L R
R D I M M B S U L I H P O E H T Z G R D N H K Z M A N A S S E H
```

John Background

Author of John: John. John's family must have been one of means and influence since he was known personally by the High Priest (John 18:15). Mark 1:20 seems to indicate that Zebedee had a successful fishing business because he used hired servants. John was a disciple of John the Baptist, and was introduced to Jesus through him (John 1:35-40). John followed Christ on His first tour of Galilee (John 1:43), where he attended the wedding feast in Cana. He was later recuited by Christ and commissioned as one of the twelve disciples. John was a member of the inner circle of apostles which included his brother James and Peter. These three accompanied Christ on some very special occasions. John also wrote First, Second and Third John, and the book of Revelation.

Date of Writing: Two major schools of thought exist concerning the dating of the Gospel of John. One group believes that John was written around A.D. 67; whereas, the other group believes John was written around A.D. 96. The second group gives the later date because of a statement made by St. Irenaeus, a church father who lived during the first century. There is considerable room for doubt about the meaning of St. Irenaeus' statement. He said that either John was alive and had been seen by other believers during Domitian's reign, or that John's prophecy in Revelation was seen by the believers during Domitian's reign. We cannot be certain of the precise meaning of St. Irenaeus' comment. In either case, St. Irenaeus was referring to the book of Revelation and not the Gospel of John.

The first group believes in the early writing of the Gospel because the implication given, as you read through John, is that the temple was still in existence at the time of writing. There is no reference to the destruction of Jerusalem and the temple, which took place in 70 A.D. If the temple had been destroyed by the time John wrote his Gospel, he most likely would have made reference to it (John 2:19-21). Although there are other factors to consider, these are the two main lines of reasoning for the dating of John's Gospel.

Purpose of John: The purpose for the book is clearly spelled out for us in John 20:31. "But these are written, that ye might believe that Jesus is the Christ, the Son of God; and that believing ye might have life through His name."

Outline of John:

I.   Period of Consideration (John 1-4)
      A.   Christ the Word (John 1)
      B.   Christ the Creator (John 2)
      C.   Christ the Savior (John 3)
      D.   Christ the Giver of Life (John 4)

II.   Period of Controversy (John 5-6)
     A.   Christ the Judge (John 5)
     B.   Christ the Bread of Life (John 6)

III.   Period of Conflict (John 7-12)
     A.   Christ the Divider (John 7)
     B.   Christ the Light of the World (John 8 & 9)
     C.   Christ the Good Shepherd (John 10)
     D.   Christ the Resurrection and the Life (John 11)
     E.   Christ the Center of Attraction (John 12)

IV.   Period of Conference (John 13-17)
     A.   Christ the Servant (John 13)
     B.   Christ the Comforter (John 14)
     C.   Christ the Vine (John 15 & 16))
     D.   Christ the Intercessor (John 17)

V.   Period of Consummation (John 18-21)
     A.   Christ the Sacrifice (John 18-19)
     B.   Christ the Victor (John 20)
     C.   Christ the Loved (John 21)

Big Idea of John: Written to present Christ and His deity, the Gospel of John depicts Christ as the Son of God. The emphasis is upon love. John has been characterized as the apostle of love.

The focus of John's Gospel centers around the defense of Christ as God's Son. When Christ said "I am" (John 8:58), the people knew that He was claiming the very name of God that was revealed to Moses at the burning bush (Ex. 3:14). Along the same line, John demonstrates how Christ asserted his deity by adding that He was the Bread of life (6:35); the Light of the world (8:12); the Door (10:7); the Good Shepherd (10:11); the Resurrection and Life (11:25); the Way, Truth and Life (14:6); and the True vine (15:1).

John is the most selective of the four Gospel writers. Over 90% of his content is unique from Matthew, Mark and Luke. Many great sermons are found only in John: the new birth (3:1-13); the water of life (4:6-29); the defense of Christ's deity (5:19-47); the Bread of life (6:22-71); the Light of the world (8:12-59); the Good Shepherd (10:1-30); and the upper room discourse (13:1-16:33).

John wrote in a very simple style. Of the four Gospels, this book is the easiest to read in the original Greek language, in which it was written.

Moral Integrity
Lesson #47

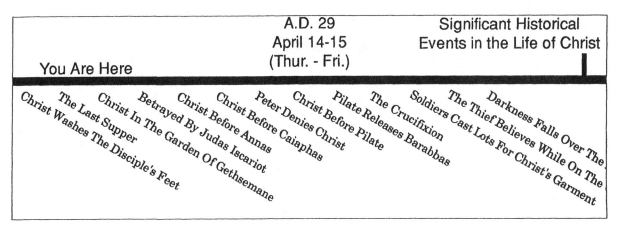

	A.D. 29 April 14-15 (Thur. - Fri.)	Significant Historical Events in the Life of Christ
You Are Here		

Christ Washes The Disciple's Feet
The Last Supper
Christ In The Garden Of Gethsemane
Betrayed By Judas Iscariot
Christ Before Annas
Christ Before Caiaphas
Peter Denies Christ
Christ Before Pilate
Pilate Releases Barabbas
The Crucifixion
Soldiers Cast Lots For Christ's Garment
The Thief Believes While On The
Darkness Falls Over The

Lesson Goal: To understand what it means to have moral integrity.

Background Text: Matthew 26:14-16; Mark 14:10-11; Luke 22:1-6

Memory Verse: For they loved the praise of men more than the praise of God. John 12:43

A true test of a person's moral character is what they do when no one else is watching. When you are alone, what do you do and think about? Are they things that would glorify or dishonor God? The things we do in private are a reflection of our moral integrity. "I will behave myself wisely in a perfect way. O when wilt thou come unto me? I will walk within my house with a perfect heart. I will set no wicked thing before mine eyes: I hate the work of them that turn aside; it shall not cleave to me." (Psalms 101:2&3)

When we talk of moral integrity, or the lack thereof, for many people the name of Judas Iscariot comes to mind. Here is the man who sold the life of our Lord for thirty silver coins. Judas should be an example to all of us that we need to maintain a standard of moral purity. It is this moral integrity that will determine our effectiveness for the Lord.

You do not need to read many newspapers or watch more than a few news programs to see that moral integrity is lacking in our society today. Judges take bribes to "fix" criminal cases; salesmen misrepresent their products to their clients; politicians lie to their constituents; businessmen cheat their employers; and employees steal from the companies for which they work. From all appearances, it seems that most people live by their own set of standards with no regard for the absolutes in God's Word.

The person who feels that regular church attendance is all that is needed to be a good Christian is sadly mistaken. As believers, it is time to take Christ to our jobs, our schools, our friends, and our neighbors. We can do this by applying the principles of God's Word to our lives and living by His holy standards.

The Bible is very specific about the standards for Christian conduct. Galatians 5:18-23, I Corinthians 6:9-10, I Corinthians 13, II Corinthians 12:21, James 3:13-18, and II Peter 1:5-11 describe what is acceptable and unacceptable Christian behavior. These standards are not merely suggestions. They are the requirements necessary to live a Godly life. Study these passages, memorize their contents and set them before you like a beacon in the night. Let them guide and direct your thoughts and actions in a world where absolutes and integrity are nearly nonexistent.

Questions:

1. Who sought opportunity to betray Jesus? (Matt. 26:14-16) _____

2. Who was Judas Iscariot? (Matt. 26:14) _____

3. What did Judas say when he went to see the chief priests? (Matt. 26:14-15)

   _____

4. What was the price that the chief priests paid for Christ's betrayal? (Matt. 26:15) _____

5. How did the chief priests feel when Judas agreed to help them? (Mark 14:11)

   _____

6. What special celebration drew nigh? (Luke 22:1) _____

_____

7. Why were the chief priests so careful in their plans to kill Jesus? (Luke 22:2)

_____

8. What caused Judas to want to betray Jesus? (Luke 22:3) _____

9. With whom did Judas talk about betraying Jesus? (Luke 22:4) _____

_____

10. When was Jesus to be betrayed? (Luke 22:6) _____

_____

Thought Questions:

1. What are some ways that we betray Jesus today? _____

_____

_____

_____

_____

_____

_____

2. What would you do if you were betrayed by one of your best friends like Jesus
   was? _____

_____

_____

_____

_____

_____

_____

Lesson Review:

1. How much money did the poor widow give? (Lesson #46) _____

2. Why are many Jews still waiting for the Messiah to come? (Lesson #44) _____

_____

_____

3. Why is it unnecessary to covet? (Lesson #39) _____

_____

_____

Humble Service
Lesson #48

29 A.D.

Capernaum ■

Sea of Galilee

■ Nazareth

Jordan River

■ Samaria

Our Lord washed the disciples' feet in the upper room within the city of Jerusalem.

■ Jerusalem

■ Bethlehem

Dead Sea

0   10   20

Scale of Miles

<u>Lesson Goal</u>: To understand the importance of humble service.

<u>Background Text</u>: Matthew 26:20-35; Mark 14:17-31; Luke 22:14-38; John 13:1-38

<u>Memory Verse</u>: Wherefore let him that thinketh he standeth take heed lest he fall. I Corinthians 10:12

In Jewish tradition, the Passover meal was a very special event. It allowed an individual to reflect upon God's goodness toward him and his family. The story of the first Passover is told in Exodus 12. This was when God commanded Pharaoh to allow the Israelites to leave Egypt. If he refused, God said that He would kill the first-born male of each family. In order to protect themselves, God's people slaughtered a lamb and placed its blood above the entrance of the door to their home. This was a sign that they trusted God and believed in His covenant. Since that night, the Jewish people have celebrated the Passover every year as a reminder of God's goodness and forbearance toward them.

Back in the Old Testament, lambs and other animals were sacrificed to God as the way to atone for sins committed. Throughout Christ's ministry, He explained to His followers that He was the final and ultimate sacrifice for sin. Christ came to die for man's sins and was sacrificed on the cross just as lambs were sacrificed upon the altars.

It was during the Passover meal that our Lord again

explained to His disciples that He must die. Although they did not understand what Christ was teaching them, He illustrated what He meant by washing their feet. Traditionally, people from this time period did not take baths or showers as often as we do today. Not only was water scarce, but they did not have an effective means of plumbing. Instead of bathing their whole bodies on a regular basis, they would wash their feet. This was necessary since most of the traveling was accomplished by walking. On the dusty paths of that time, an individual's feet would become quite dirty as he walked from one place to another.

When it came time for the Passover supper, rather than the men washing their own feet, Christ did it for them. By doing this, He was humbling Himself before them as their Servant. This was a sign to the disciples that as their Servant, He was going to suffer and die for their sins. Just as He cleansed their feet of dirt, He was about to cleanse their hearts of sin.

As Christ explained this to His disciples, He also added that they were to humbly serve one another. We are not to let pride stand in the way of Godly actions. Christ, who was greater, served those who were lesser. This example was given to us by our Lord so that we could lay aside our own rank and esteem and serve our brethren. Through these humble efforts the love of a Christian grows, and the church of Christ is strengthened.

Questions: Please indicate your answer with either True or False.

1. _____ Jesus said that one of His disciples would betray Him. (Matt. 26:20-21)

2. _____ No one was upset at Christ's statement. (Matt. 26:22)

3. _____ Jesus said that the one who would betray Him was the one that dippeth his hand with Him in the dish. (Matt. 26:23)

4. _____ The bread that Jesus broke represented His blood. (Matt. 26:26)

5. _____ The cup represented Christ's body. (Mark 14:23-24)

6. _____ When they had sung a hymn they went to the Mount of Olives. (Mark 14:26)

7. _____ The disciples argued over who was the greatest. (Luke 22:24)

8. _____ Jesus warned Simon that Satan had a desire to sift him like wheat. (Luke 22:31)

9. _____ Jesus said that Peter would deny Him four times. (Luke 22:34)

10. _____ Jesus washed the disciples' feet. (John 13:5)

Thought Questions:

1. What is something that you can specifically do to serve someone today? _____

_____

_____

_____

Humble Service

2. What are some things that you can do to be a servant to your parents every day? _____

_____

_____

_____

_____

Lesson Review:

1. What is a true test of a person's moral character? (Lesson #47) _____

_____

_____

_____

2. For how much did Judas Iscariot betray Jesus? (Lesson #47) _____

_____

3. What was the rich young ruler unwilling to do? (Lesson #46) _____

_____

Supplemental Exercise: Translate this Greek passage from John 3:16 into English. The dictionary can be found in Appendix C.

ουτως γαρ ηγαπησεν ο θεος

_____

τον κοσμον ωστε τον υιον

_____

τον μονογενη ινα πας

_____

ο πιστευων εις αυτον

_____

μη αποληται αλλ εχη ζωην αιωνιον

_____

The Suffering Savior
Lesson #49

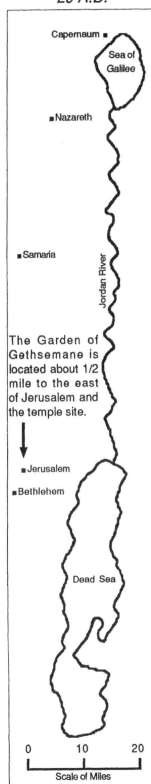

29 A.D.

Capernaum ■

Sea of Galilee

■ Nazareth

■ Samaria

Jordan River

The Garden of Gethsemane is located about 1/2 mile to the east of Jerusalem and the temple site.

■ Jerusalem

■ Bethlehem

Dead Sea

0   10   20

Scale of Miles

Lesson Goal: To understand the suffering our Lord experienced at Gethsemane.

Background Text: Matthew 26:36-46; Mark 14:32-42; Luke 22:39-46; John 18:1-4

Memory Verse: Watch and pray, that ye enter not into temptation: the spirit indeed is willing, but the flesh is weak. Matthew 26:41

It is difficult to imagine the pain and suffering our Lord must have experienced prior to His arrest and crucifixion. Luke writes that while praying in the Garden of Gethsemane, Christ sweat drops of blood. So intense was His suffering and grief that His physical system was in turmoil.

Some people question how Christ, as God, could have experienced such great distress. The answer lies in the fact that Christ, along with being fully God, was also fully man. The humanity of Christ that allowed Him to hunger, thirst, and be tempted, also allowed Him to grieve. When Christ asked His heavenly Father, "Let this cup pass from me," He was not rebelling against the will of God. He was simply admitting that He recognized how difficult His death would be, and wondered if there was any other alternative.

The grief that Christ experienced was focused in two directions. First, our Lord dreaded the pain and suffering He would endure on the road to Calvary. He knew the horrible torture that awaited Him at the hands of some very cruel people. Imagine how you would feel if someone told you that within the next twenty-four hours you would be beaten, whipped, stuck with thorns, nailed to a piece of wood, and left to suffocate and slowly die! Needless to say, you would not look forward to it with glee and delight. Most likely you would do all in your power to avoid that kind of suffering.

The second reason that Christ was grieved was that He knew that in dying for the sins of man, He would be rejected

The Suffering Savior

by His heavenly Father. While on the cross, God the Father forsook His Son because He viewed Christ as a sinner. In order to atone for man's sin, Christ, who knew no sin Himself, became the offering to God (II Corinthians 5:21). By accepting the sin upon Himself, Christ lost fellowship with God. This fellowship was later restored when Christ triumphed over sin and death by His resurrection.

Let this be a lesson to us. Christ suffered so that we would not experience the eternal consequences of our own sin. If you ever doubt Christ's love, then consider that He suffered and died specifically for you. This love was demonstrated so that you, by believing in Christ as your Lord and Savior, could have eternal life.

Questions: Multiple choice -- circle the correct answer for each question.

1. Where did Jesus take His disciples? (Matt. 26:36)
   *Rome
   *Gethsemane
   *Israel
   *Samaria

2. Who did He take with Him to pray? (Matt. 26:37)
   *Matthew and John the Baptist
   *Paul, Peter and John
   *Peter and the sons of Zebedee
   *Peter, Philip and Judas Iscariot

3. What did Jesus ask of the Father? (Matt. 26:39)
   *That He would continue to be with Him
   *That He would take the cup from Him
   *That there would be no pain in His death
   *That His death would come quickly

4. What did He find His disciples doing? (Matt. 26:43)
   *Sleeping
   *Praying
   *Eating
   *Watching the sunset

5. The spirit is ready but the flesh is what? (Mark 14:38)
   *Strong
   *Dead
   *Weak
   *Alive

6. How many times did Jesus find His disciples sleeping? (Mark 14:41)
    *Five times
    *Three times
    *Two times
    *Four times

7. Into what was the Son of Man betrayed? (Mark 14:41)
    *The hands of the sinners
    *The hands of the righteous
    *The hands of the poor
    *The hands of the just

8. They were to pray so as not to enter what? (Luke 22:40)
    *Doubt
    *Security
    *Death
    *Temptation

9. How far was Jesus from them? (Luke 22:41)
    *A stone's cast
    *Over the hill
    *A mile away
    *In the next garden

10. Over what brook did Jesus and His disciples go? (John 18:1)
    *Cherith
    *Cedron
    *Kidron
    *Kishon

Thought Questions:

1. Why do you believe it was necessary for Christ to suffer for man's sin? Why could He not have just died a simple death? _____

    _____

    _____

    _____

    _____

2. How have you suffered or been persecuted for the Lord Jesus? List an example or two. _____

    _____

    _____

    _____

    _____

The Suffering Savior

Lesson Review:

1. Why was the Passover meal a special event? (Lesson #48) _____

_____

_____

2. What was the purpose of the Gospel of John? (John Background) _____

_____

_____

Supplemental Exercise: Solve the logic problem.

Boaz, the camel trader, had just received a new shipment of camels from a neighboring country. On the very first day he had the new camels he sold five. From the information given, determine who bought what camel, in what order they were sold, and the cost of each one.

1. The single hump which cost $3.00 less than the one Caleb bought, was purchased last, just after the least expensive.

2. David chose the most expensive camel. Matthew bought the racing camel, but he was not the second to buy a camel today.

3. Caleb bought his camel first.   It was not the spitting camel

4. Joshua's camel costs $4.00 more than the plowing camel.

	Single hump	Double hump	Spitting	Racing	Plowing	First	Second	Third	Fourth	Fifth	$62	$65	$66	$69	$73
Aaron															
Caleb															
David															
Matthew															
Joshua															
$62															
$65															
$66															
$69															
$73															
First															
Second															
Third															
Fourth															
Fifth															

The Trial of Christ
Lesson #50

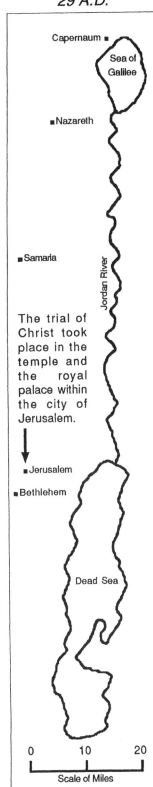

29 A.D.

Capernaum

Sea of Galilee

Nazareth

Samaria

Jordan River

The trial of Christ took place in the temple and the royal palace within the city of Jerusalem.

Jerusalem

Bethlehem

Dead Sea

0   10   20

Scale of Miles

<u>Lesson Goal</u>: To understand that Christ was condemned as an innocent man.

<u>Background Text</u>: Matthew 26:57-27:26; Mark 14:53-15:15; Luke 22:54-23:25; John 18:13-19:16

<u>Memory Verse</u>: And this is the condemnation, that light is come into the world, and men love darkness rather than light, because their deeds were evil. For every one that doeth evil hateth the light, neither cometh to the light, lest his deeds should be reproved. John 3:19-20

Have you ever been blamed for doing something that you did not do? It is very frustrating, isn't it? As a father, I need to be very careful that before I punish one of my children, I am certain that I discipline the one who actually deserves it.

None of us would want to be accused of being unjust. This is one of the reasons that we have a legal system in this country which says, "Innocent until proven guilty." When the court tries someone for a crime, there has to be enough evidence against him to prove that he is guilty beyond a reasonable doubt.

Unfortunately for our Lord, what was supposed to be a trial was only a way for the Jewish leaders to condemn Christ. Remember that most of the Pharisees and Sadducees hated Jesus since He spoke against their ridiculous legalistic system of adding to the Law of Moses. In order to keep the people from following Christ and believing His message, the leaders sought to have our Lord put to death.

There was no way that the Pharisees and Sadducees could honestly condemn Christ. He had never sinned, and therefore had never broken any of God's laws. The only thing the Jews could do was lie about Christ and bring up false witnesses to testify against Him. Christ was falsely accused of doing something He never did.

A few days earlier, when our Lord rode into Jerusalem on a

donkey, He was welcomed by the people as their King. They expected Jesus to free them from the oppressive Roman government. Although they did not understand that Christ came to be their spiritual King, they eventually realized that He was not going to fight against the Romans. As a result, the people did not want to have anything to do with our Lord. Since they had forgotten His miracles and everything He had taught, they went along with the unrighteous plans of Caiaphas to have Christ crucified.

As believers, there will be times when the world will misunderstand our message and lie about us. Many people do not appreciate the mystery of the Gospel and the love of the Lord Jesus Christ. Society, with all its pagan practices, desires to hurt the true believer because it is unwilling to accept God's moral absolutes and the principles of the Bible. Our memory verse for this lesson reminds us that men love the darkness and the practice of wickedness because the light of God's Word convicts them of their sin.

Christ tells us in Matthew 5:12 to rejoice when persecuted because our reward in heaven will be great, for so they persecuted the prophets who were before us. We can rejoice because we know that not only has Christ suffered for us, but He has also provided a place for us in heaven where we will share eternity with Him.

Questions:

1. To what High Priest did they lead Jesus? (Matt. 26:57) _____

_____

2. By when did Peter deny Jesus three times? (Matt. 26:75) _____

_____

3. To whom did the chief priests and elders take Jesus? (Matt. 27:2) _____

_____

4. What did Judas Iscariot do with the thirty pieces of silver? (Matt. 27:3-5) ____

_____

_____

5. What was the custom of the feast? (Mark 15:6) _____

_____

6. What did Barabbas do? (Mark 15:7) _____
_____

7. To whom did Pilate send Jesus? (Luke 23:6-7) _____

8. Even though Pilate and Herod found Jesus to be innocent, what did the people want? (Luke 23:21) _____
_____

9. What did the people say to Pilate when He sought to release Jesus? (John 19:12) _____
_____

10. What is the place of the judgment seat called in Hebrew? (John 19:13) _____
_____

Thought Questions:

1. Why do you think God tells us to rejoice when we are persecuted? _____
_____
_____
_____
_____
_____
_____

2. How do you rejoice when you are persecuted? _____
_____
_____
_____
_____
_____

Lesson Review:

1. In what two directions was the grief of Christ focused? (Lesson #49) _____
_____
_____

2. How many lepers returned to thank Christ for healing them? (Lesson #42) ___
_____

3. Whom did Jesus come to call? (Lesson #19) _____
_____
_____

The Crucifixion of Christ
Lesson #51

29 A.D.

Capernaum

Sea of Galilee

Nazareth

Samaria

Jordan River

Golgotha, the place where Christ was crucified, is located in the northwest section of Jerusalem.

Jerusalem

Bethlehem

Dead Sea

0   10   20

Scale of Miles

Lesson Goal: To understand that the crucifixion was the final atonement for sin and nullified the Old Testament sacrificial system.

Background Text: Matthew 27:31-66; Mark 15:20-47; Luke 23:26-56; John 19:16-42

Memory Verse: Christ hath redeemed us from the curse of the law, being made a curse for us: for it is written, "Cursed is every one that hangeth on a tree." Galatians 3:13

Throughout history, man has been in a never-ending battle against sin and its consequences. Wars have been fought, people have died, societies have been ruined – all as a result of the curse of sin. God, in His infinite wisdom, knew that in order for sin to be forgiven, a sacrifice had to be made. For several thousand years, man practiced the killing of animals as the means of atonement and forgiveness for their sins. This was only a temporary remedy, since their sins were forgiven only for a short time. Year after year, sacrifices had to be made because the blood of animals could not take away sin.

When the fullness of time came, God provided the ultimate sacrifice to wash away man's sins (Galatians 4:4-5). He

gave us His only Son to suffer, shed His blood, and die. Had it not been for the death of our Lord, we would still be living by the Old Testament sacrificial system. However, Christ's death fulfilled the Law and its requirements. Paul says in Galatians 3:24, "Wherefore the law was our schoolmaster to bring us unto Christ, that we might be justified by faith."

At the moment of Christ's death, several things happened as recorded in Matthew 27:51-54. One of those things was the temple veil being torn into two pieces. As part of the requirement of the Law, the temple veil separated the Holy of Holies from the Holy Place. Once a year the High Priest would go beyond the veil into the Holy of Holies and make atonement for the sins of the people. The veil separated the presence of God from the rest of the priests who performed their daily duties in the Holy Place. This separation was necessary because man was unable to come to God directly since his unforgiven sin could not be in contact with the holiness of God.

Through His death, Christ became the mediator between God and man (I Timothy 2:5). We as believers can now come directly to God through Christ because His death cleansed and purified us from sin. The temple veil was torn because, in the eyes of God, it was no longer necessary. Christ took the place of the veil.

Some people have said that all religions lead to God. According to them, it does not matter who or what you believe. As long as you have faith in something and do good, you will go to heaven. To those people I ask, "Was Buddha, Mohammad, or anyone else for that matter, the perfect sacrifice and capable of dying for our sins?" No! Then how can belief in these individuals lead us to God? It cannot!

Christ's death was significant because it provided the only way for man to get to God. Our Lord, during His ministry, said, "I am the way, the truth, and the life," "I am the good shepherd," "I am the door," "I am the vine... abide in me." Christ was not saying these words for His benefit, but for ours. Christ gave His life so that we may have eternal life. Now it is our responsibility to believe and receive Him as the Lord and Savior of our lives.

Questions: Multiple choice -- circle the correct answer for each question.

1. Who was forced to carry Christ's cross? (Matt. 27:32)
    *Jesus
    *Peter
    *Simon
    *A Roman soldier

2. Where was Jesus crucified? (Matt. 27:33-35)
    *Golgotha
    *Nazareth
    *Rome
    *Bethlehem

3. What was written over Christ's head? (Matt. 27:37)
    *He called Himself the King of the Jews.
    *This is Jesus the King of the Jews.
    *This man deserves to die.
    *He saved others but He could not save Himself.

4. What did Jesus say He could destroy? (Matt. 27:40)
    *The Roman empire
    *The temple
    *Sinners
    *The world

5. Who were the two men crucified with Jesus? (Mark 15:27)
    *Peter and John
    *Murderers
    *Common thieves
    *Priests

6. At what hour did darkness first cover the land? (Mark 15:33)
    *The sixteenth hour
    *The ninth hour
    *The third hour
    *The sixth hour

7. At the cross, who confessed that Jesus was God's Son? (Mark 15:39)
    *Mary Magdalene
    *The centurion
    *Pontius Pilate
    *Herod

8. For whom did Jesus tell the women to weep? (Luke 23:28)
    *The nation of Israel
    *God
    *His disciples
    *Themselves and their children

9. What did the people give Jesus to drink? (John 19:29)
    *Water
    *Wine
    *Vinegar
    *Milk

10. Who took the body of Jesus and buried it? (John 19:38)
    *Joseph, Christ's father
    *Joseph of Arimathea
    *Peter
    *Mary Magdalene

Thought Questions:

1. How does Christ's death and resurrection save us from our sins? _____
_____
_____
_____
_____

2. Why is it necessary that we believe upon the Lord Jesus Christ for our salvation and not upon anyone or anything else? _____
_____
_____
_____
_____

3. How would you explain to a non-Christian that they need to believe in Christ Jesus in order to receive eternal life? _____
_____
_____
_____
_____
_____

Lesson Review:

1. Why did the Jews turn against Christ? (Lesson #50) _____
_____
_____

2. Why does the world sometimes misunderstand the Gospel message? (Lesson #50) _____
_____

3. When Christ told the parable of the widow's offering, about what was He speaking? (Lesson #46) _____
_____

Lord-Legend-Lunatic-Liar
Lesson #52

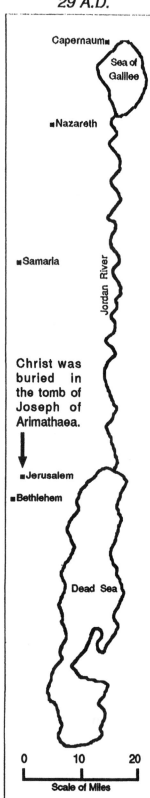

29 A.D.

Capernaum

Sea of Galilee

Nazareth

Samaria

Jordan River

Christ was buried in the tomb of Joseph of Arimathaea.

Jerusalem

Bethlehem

Dead Sea

0   10   20

Scale of Miles

Lesson Goal: To understand the evidence that points to the deity and lordship of Christ.

Background Text: Matthew 28:1-7; Mark 16:1-7; Luke 24:1-8; John 20:1-2

Memory Verse: Jesus said unto her, I am the resurrection, and the life: he that believeth in me, though he were dead, yet shall he live. John 11:25

When we consider the evidence of the resurrection and the historical person of Jesus Christ, our conclusion can go in one of four directions. Josh McDowell, in his book <u>Evidence that Demands a Verdict</u>, explains that our conclusion will be that Christ was either the Lord, a legend, a lunatic, or a liar.

Did Christ lie about who He was in order to deceive His followers? There are not many people who believe this; otherwise, why would Christ have suffered a terrible death at the hands of the Romans? If He had lied about being God's Son, He could have simply renounced His claim to deity while on trial before Pilate and then been set free.

If Christ did not lie about who He was, perhaps He was a lunatic, a madman, who only thought that He was God's Son. The trouble with this line of reasoning is that nowhere in the Gospels does Christ exhibit any unusual or abnormal behavior. One would think that if Christ were insane, He would have acted strangely around His disciples. In addition, there is no way to account for all the miracles performed by Christ. Too many people who followed Christ saw Him perform a variety of miracles. Perhaps a few people could have been deceived, but not everyone.

Most non-Christians believe that Christ was a good teacher and a moral leader, but possessed no divine attributes. These people feel that after the death of our Lord, the disciples and writers of the Gospels developed the myth concerning Christ, that He was actually God's Son. In other words, the writers of the Gospels made up stories about things that Christ never said or did. This view holds Christ to be just a legend.

Upon closer examination of this theory several problems arise. First of all, how could ordinary men, who were mostly fishermen, develop such a complex and diverse theology? Most of these individuals had no formal schooling. The unique concept of the two natures (God and man) in one person would be almost impossible to invent and explain.

Next, why would a group of men, if deceiving the world, sacrifice their lives for something that they knew was false? They could not all have been insane! What could possibly motivate them to dream up the idea of a Messiah who no one wanted and for whom they would be willing to die?

Finally, these individuals did not seek to profit or gain anything for their own interests. The followers of Christ, as a whole, were a financially poor group of people. They did not have much in the way of material possessions. Most con-artists deceive people so they can steal their money and get rich. The disciples had no reason to deceive the people since they did not gain anything in return.

There is only one proper conclusion that we can gather about Jesus Christ. If Christ was not a liar, lunatic or legend, then He must have been who He said He was, the Lord of all and the Son of God. If this is true, then what He preached must also be true. As God's Son, our Lord proclaimed that no one could come to the Father except through Him. Those who reject the Lordship of Christ lose all hope of eternal life.

There are things in our lives that we believe because someone has told them to us and they make sense. Then there are things we believe only after we have carefully studied the facts and come to accept them as truth. The resurrection and person of Jesus Christ must fall into this second category. When it comes to our belief in God, it is important to know what we believe, why we believe it and then be able to defend the reason we believe that way. This is so necessary to understand; otherwise, our faith and trust in God may weaken when Satan tempts us and throws doubts in our direction.

<u>Questions</u>: Please indicate your answer with either True or False.

1. _____ Mary Magdalene and the other Mary came to see the sepulchre at the end of the Sabbath on the second day of the week. (Matt. 28:1)

2. _____ Before the angel appeared there was a great thunderstorm. (Matt. 28:2)

Lord-Legend-Lunatic-Liar

3. _____ The angel stood in front of the grave because God did not give him the power to open the grave. (Matt. 28:2)

4. _____ His raiment was white as wool. (Matt. 28:3)

5. _____ The women brought with them clothes in which to wrap the body of Jesus. (Mark. 16:1)

6. _____ God gave the women power to roll away the stone from the grave. (Mark 16:1-3)

7. _____ The angel told them to be afraid because Jesus had risen. (Mark 16:6)

8. _____ When the angel reminded the women of Christ's words, they still did not remember that Jesus had ever said these words. (Luke 24:8)

9. _____ The women went to the twelve disciples to tell them what they had seen. (Luke 24:9)

10. _____ Mary Magdalene went to James and John to tell them the news. (John 20:2)

Thought Questions:

1. How does the resurrection of Christ set Christianity apart from any other religion? _____

_____

_____

_____

_____

_____

2. Why do you think people deny the resurrection of Christ Jesus? _____

_____

_____

_____

_____

_____

Lesson Review:

1. Explain why the temple veil was torn in two. (Lesson #51) _____

_____

_____

_____

2. Why could the Pharisees and Sadducees not honestly condemn Christ? (Lesson #50) _____

_____

_____

3. Why did God forsake Christ while He was on the cross? (Lesson #49) _____

_____

Supplemental Exercise: Solve the logic problem.

During the time of Christ, children did not have the luxury to go to a store and buy a toy whenever they wanted. Instead, they would play by using their imagination and making toys of their own. Judah and four other children decide to each make a special toy to give as a gift to the orphanage. One is building a boat. Each child is particularly gifted in the use of one tool. From the clues listed can you determine which tool each child uses best and what gift each child is making?

1. The five children are Judah, the one making the birdhouse, the one making a rag doll and the ones most adept with the plane and the knife.

2. Those skillful with the mallet and the saw are both boys; the third boy is making a whistle.

3. Job is making a gift for the first time, but those making the whistle and the rag doll have made gifts before.

4. Judah is not making a model chariot.

5. Miriam's speciality is not the chisel.

6. Using the knife is not the speciality of the whistle maker.

7. The mallet, which is not being used on the birdhouse, is not Dan's speciality.

	Mallet	Chisel	Saw	Knife	Plane	Birdhouse	Whistle	Chariot	Rag Doll	Boat
Judah										
Rebekah										
Job										
Miriam										
Dan										
Birdhouse										
Whistle										
Chariot										
Rag Doll										
Boat										

The Joy of the Resurrection
Lesson #53

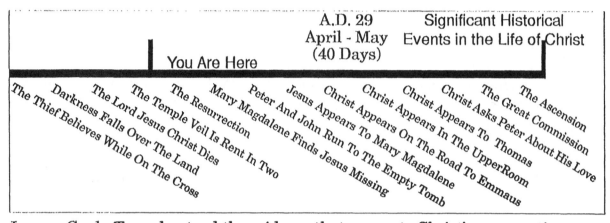

A.D. 29
April - May
(40 Days)

Significant Historical
Events in the Life of Christ

You Are Here

The Thief Believes While On The Cross
The Darkness Falls Over The Land
The Lord Jesus Christ Dies
The Temple Veil Is Rent In Two
The Resurrection
Mary Magdalene Finds Jesus Missing
Peter And John Run To The Empty Tomb
Jesus Appears To Mary Magdalene
Christ Appears On The Road To Emmaus
Christ Appears In The UpperRoom
Christ Appears To Thomas
Christ Asks Peter About His Love
The Great Commission
The Ascension

<u>Lesson Goal</u>: To understand the evidence that supports Christ's resurrection.

<u>Background Text</u>: Matthew 28:8-15; Mark 16:8-11; Luke 24:9-12; John 20:3-18

<u>Memory Verse</u>: Jesus said unto her, I am the resurrection, and the life; he that believeth in me, though he were dead, yet shall he live. John 11:25

No other event in the history of mankind is as significant as the resurrection of Jesus Christ. Even our Lord's birth and death fade in comparison to the resurrection, since by it Christ conquered sin and provided a means of eternal life with God the Father.

Think about this for a moment: had it not been for the resurrection of Christ, our faith would be hopeless. We would have no forgiveness of sins, no permanent atonement, no justification with the Father and no fellowship with God. If you take away the resurrection of our Lord Jesus Christ, you remove the basic ingredient of Christianity. Little wonder why so many pagans deny the resurrection of our Lord, for by the resurrection Christianity stands or falls.

Unlike any other religion or system of belief, we serve a risen Lord and Savior. This was the joy of discovery that the women and later the disciples experienced when they met the risen Savior. All of a sudden the things that Christ had

taught the disciples about destroying the temple and rebuilding it in three days made sense (Matthew 26:61). The covenantal sacrificial system had been destroyed and replaced by the new covenant.

When we consider the events of Christ's resurrection, we have to ask ourselves how we know this actually happened. It is important, as Christians, that we study the facts and issues behind the things that we believe, including the basis of our faith. I Peter 3:15 says to always be ready to give an answer for the things that we believe. This means that like a good lawyer, we need to defend that which we hold to be true.

There are three lines of reasoning to support the miraculous resurrection of Christ Jesus. The first piece of evidence is that of the empty tomb. Something had to have happened to the body of Christ. Either it was removed by someone else, or it left by itself. The reason that it is not acceptable to believe that someone stole the body is that they would be unable to get it past the Roman soldiers who guarded the tomb. According to the military customs of that time, a Roman guard consisted of twelve to sixteen well-trained and heavily-armed individuals. Since failure to perform a given duty was punishable by death, there was no way these soldiers were going to allow anyone to remove the body of Christ.

The next piece of evidence to support the resurrection of Christ was His appearance to more then five hundred individuals after His death (I Corinthians 15:6). There is not much of a chance that an impostor could have tricked all these people.

Finally, consider the results and reactions of the followers of Christ. The resurrection changed individuals who were cowards at the time of Christ's death into courageous men who went into all the world to share with others the Gospel of Christ. This would not have happened if they did not actually believe that Christ had risen from the dead.

The resurrection of Christ has been changing the hearts and lives of those who trust in Him for the past two thousand years. Even though what we believe affects how we feel and what we trust, our salvation does not result from storing away facts and figures concerning the Bible. We teach the facts of the resurrection in order to understand its truthfulness, but it is not enough to believe in facts alone. Take this knowledge, apply it to your belief, and allow it to grow and strengthen your walk with God. The goal of education and the objective of learning is to become a better person so that we can bring glory to our Lord and Creator.

The Joy of the Resurrection

<u>Questions:</u>

1. And they departed quickly from the sepulchre with fear and great _____;
   and did run to bring His _____ word. (Matt. 28:8)

2. And as they went to tell His disciples, behold _____ met them saying
   _____, and they came and held Him by the feet and
   _____ Him. (Matt. 28:9)

3. Then Jesus said to them, be not _____. (Matt. 28:10)

4. And when they were assembled with the _____, and had taken counsel,
   they gave large _____ unto the _____. (Matt. 28:12)

5. Saying, say ye, His _____ came by night and _____ Him
   away while we _____. (Matt. 28:13)

6. And they went out quickly and fled from the _____; for they
   _____ and were _____: neither said they anything
   to any man; for they were _____. (Mark 16:8)

7. Now when Jesus was risen early the _____ day of the week, He appeared
   first to _____, out of whom He had cast _____
   devils. (Mark 16:9)

8. And their words seemed to them as _____ tales and they _____
   them not. (Luke 24:11)

9. Then arose _____, and ran unto the _____; and stooping
   down, he beheld the _____ clothes laid by themselves and departed
   _____ in himself at that which was come to pass. (Luke 24:12)

10. _____ saith to her, Touch me not; for I am not yet _____
    to my father: but go to my _____, and say unto them, I ascend
    unto my _____, and your _____; and to my _____,
    and your _____. (John 20:17)

<u>Thought Questions:</u>

1. Would Christianity have been different from any other religion if Christ had
   not risen from the dead? Explain your answer. _____
   _____
   _____
   _____
   _____
   _____

2. Describe how you would have felt if you were one of the disciples who saw Christ after His resurrection. _____

_____

_____

_____

Lesson Review:

1. What are the four conclusions to which a person can come regarding the resurrection of Christ Jesus? (Lesson #52) _____

_____

_____

_____

2. Why is it important to understand the facts concerning something that you believe? (Lesson #52) _____

_____

_____

3. How do we know if God, angels, heaven, and hell actually exist? (Lesson #25)

_____

_____

_____

Supplemental Exercise: Translate this Greek passage from John 15:13 into English. The dictionary can be found in Appendix C.

μειζονα ταυτης αγαπην ουδεις εχει

_____

ινα τις την ψυχην αυτου θη υπερ

_____

των φιλων αυτου

_____

The Road to Emmaus
Lesson #54

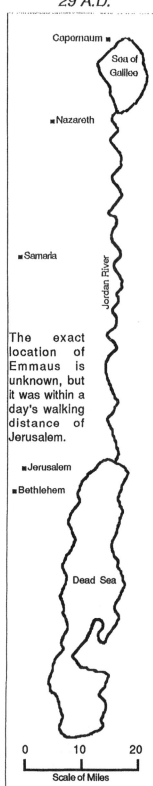

29 A.D.

Capernaum

Sea of Galilee

Nazareth

Samaria

Jordan River

The exact location of Emmaus is unknown, but it was within a day's walking distance of Jerusalem.

Jerusalem

Bethlehem

Dead Sea

0   10   20

Scale of Miles

<u>Lesson Goal</u>: To understand that wherever we go, our Lord is there with us.

<u>Background Text</u>: Mark 16:12-13; Luke 24:13-35

<u>Memory Verse</u>: And I will pray the Father, and He shall give you another Comforter, that He may abide with you forever. John 14:16

Once again, the Gospel of Luke provides evidence for the resurrection of our Lord by relating the story of Christ's appearance upon the road to Emmaus. Instead of simply saying that this person or that person saw the Lord Jesus after His resurrection, Luke gives a detailed account of this episode because of its uniqueness.

Imagine what it would be like if you were walking down the street or riding in a car when, all of a sudden, Jesus was right beside you! I think that it would be a shock to most of us. No doubt we would try to put on our best behavior and act good, so as not to embarrass ourselves. Funny thing isn't it, that we become so concerned about what other people think when they are around us, but we do not often consider what Christ thinks even though He is continually with us?

One of the greatest promises that Christ gave to His followers before He ascended into heaven was that He would send the Comforter. John 14:16 and 26 explains that after Christ's ascension, the Holy Spirit would come and indwell the lives of the believers. Today, this promise continues with us as partakers in His covenant instituted through the church. Whenever a person trusts upon the Lord Jesus as their Savior, the Holy Spirit indwells and seals him, thereby making him a permanent member of God's family.

As God's children, we have the indwelling of the Holy Spirit so we never have to worry about being alone. Ephesians 1:13 says "In whom ye also trusted, after that ye heard the word of truth, the gospel of your salvation: in whom also

after that ye believed, ye were sealed with that Holy Spirit of promise." It is important for us to realize that this third person of the Trinity is constantly with us, guiding and directing, protecting and strengthening. This indwelling will enable us to go into all the world preaching the gospel and making disciples.

Walk in a manner worthy of God,
For Christ is at your side.
The path may be long, steep and dark,
But there is no need to hide.

On the way to Emmaus with a friend and Cleopas,
The Lord Jesus suddenly appeared.
At first a stranger then later the Savior,
While at supper the two revered.

We walk our own path steadfast and true,
not always knowing the way.
Still our trust is in God and the promise of His word,
That God is with us each day.

Fear the Lord and study His Word
That by understanding you will see,
That Christ is walking next to you
As one of the Trinity.

Questions: Multiple choice -- circle the correct answer for each question.

1. How did Jesus appear unto the two men? (Mark 16:12)
    *As a light
    *As a voice
    *As a ghost
    *In another form

2. Toward what village were the two men heading?
    (Luke 24:13)
    *Antioch
    *Emmaus
    *Ephesus
    *Galilee

3. How far was this village from Jerusalem? (Luke 24:13)
   *Threescore furlongs
   *Threescore fathoms
   *Fourscore furlongs
   *A day's journey

4. What was the name of one of the men? (Luke 24:18)
   *Jezreel
   *Cleopas
   *Cappadocia
   *Chorazin

5. About what were the men sad? (Luke 24:19-20)
   *How long the journey would take
   *That they had missed their lunch
   *That Jesus was killed by the chief priests and rulers
   *They realized that the Romans would soon take power over Israel

6. Of what did the women have a vision? (Luke 24:23)
   *Angels
   *Satan
   *Men
   *The Holy Spirit

7. What part of the Scriptures did Christ start with to explain why these events
   had to come to pass? (Luke 24:27)
   *Moses and the prophets
   *Isaiah
   *Malachi
   *The Psalms

8. What did the men ask Jesus to do? (Luke 24:29)
   *To turn water into wine
   *To turn stone into bread
   *To heal their mother
   *To stay with them the evening

9. When were their eyes opened? (Luke 24:30-31)
   *When Jesus gave them bread
   *The next morning
   *When the Holy Spirit came upon them
   *When they died

10. Where did these two men go when their eyes were opened? (Luke 24:33)
    *Galilee
    *Judea
    *Jerusalem
    *Emmaus

Thought Questions:

1. Why do you think it was necessary for God to send the Holy Spirit? _____

_____

_____

_____

2. How does the Holy Spirit guide you in the decisions that you make? _____

_____

_____

Lesson Review:

1. What are the three lines of reasoning to support the resurrection of Christ Jesus? (Lesson #53) _____

_____

_____

2. To how many individuals did Christ appear after His resurrection? (Lesson #53) _____

3. Why is it unlikely that Jesus deceived His followers? (Lesson #52) _____

_____

_____

Supplemental Exercise: Unscramble the five words listed below. Take the letters that are circled and rearrange them to solve the missing phrase. Clue: the missing phrase is from this lesson's story.

DUMNEOMC

SHIDEVNA

FICDIUCER

REECHROSTE

HLRSPUEEC

_ _

Peter's Denial and Love
Lesson #55

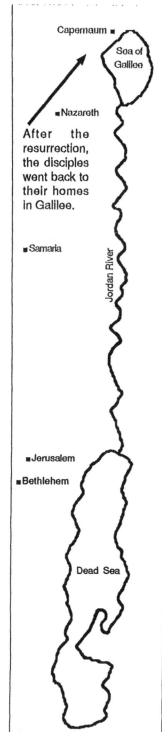

29 A.D.

Capernaum ■

Sea of Galilee

■ Nazareth

After the resurrection, the disciples went back to their homes in Galilee.

■ Samaria

Jordan River

■ Jerusalem

■ Bethlehem

Dead Sea

0   10   20

Scale of Miles

<u>Lesson Goal</u>: To understand how to cope with our failures.

<u>Background Text</u>: Matthew 26:69-75; Mark 14:66-72; Luke 22:54-62; John 18:15-27, 21:15-25

<u>Memory Verse</u>: He that soweth iniquity shall reap vanity: and the rod of his anger shall fail. Proverbs 22:8

Although it is important to study how not to fail, we also need to learn how to deal with our failure once we have failed. One common characteristic that all humans have is that, from time to time, they fail. Whether it be failing a test, failing in a business venture, failing with a relationship, or failing spiritually, failure is going to happen to all of us. My father used to tell me, "Don't be afraid to fail. The person who never failed never tried to do anything." My boss says almost the same thing: "The person who never makes mistakes or fails isn't working."

It is important to understand that not all failure is sin. If I were to fly an airplane I would fail miserably, but I would not necessarily be sinning. I have never learned how to fly, so any attempt would end in disaster. However, many failures can be avoided by following the principles of God's Word. The Bible is available to believers as a map to guide our way, so that we can avoid sinning and making mistakes. Whether our failure is a result of sin or an unforeseen accident, we still need to learn how to handle the loss, embarrassment, pressure, guilt and many other emotions that accompany the failure.

In order to cope with our failures we need to identify, prioritize, rectify and recognize. The first step in dealing with failure is to identify exactly what we did. What happened when we failed? Why did it happen? How did it happen? When we fail, we need to take a long, hard look at what we did, learn from it, and try to avoid it in the future. People can go to two different extremes in this respect. They can either ignore the problem and do nothing about it, or they can become depressed over it and allow it to ruin their lives. Neither one of these extremes is acceptable.

After you have determined the area in which you failed, you need to prioritize the failure. In the financial investment field, to prioritize is to re-evaluate where you have your money invested, and if necessary, cut your losses by moving your money into a different investment. It sometimes may be necessary to move your money from one investment, that is doing poorly, into another that is doing better. Let us say for example that no matter how hard I try to be a good chess player, I always lose. Perhaps it would be better to try something different than to go on learning the game of chess. There may be many things that each of us do very well, and many things that we do not do well. The trick is to cut our losses and concentrate our effort upon that which we do well so as to improve. We may also need to improve upon the things that we do not do well, but in the meantime accept the fact that we may experience failure in the process.

Sometimes when we fail, the consequences of that failure may extend beyond ourselves to those who are around us. Now, not being a good chess player may not affect anyone besides our opponent. However, the results of David's sin with Bathsheba affected the entire nation of Israel. When our failure results in negative consequences, we need to take the necessary step of restitution in order to rectify the situation. If we have sinned, we will need to confess the sin. If we have stolen something, we will need to pay it back. If we have hurt someone, we will need to seek their forgiveness. Whatever it is that we have done wrong, we need to do everything in our power to make it right.

Finally, we need to recognize that good will come as a result of our failure. What could appear to us as a failure, may actually be a way for God to test us and improve our character. God can use our failure to teach us things that we would not have learned had we not failed. This is why we need to be responsive to our Lord's teaching by learning from it instead of becoming so depressed and confused that we are unable to look beyond our shortcomings. There will be times when we all are going to fail, but if we can maintain the proper attitude by looking at the failure, learning from it and then growing through it, we can develop and conform our character into the fashion of Christ Jesus. "Nevertheless my lovingkindness will I not utterly take from him, nor suffer my faithfulness to fail." (Psalms 89:33)

Questions:

1. Who came to Peter when he was in the palace? (Matt. 26:69) _____

_____

2. What was Peter's answer to her statement? (Matt. 26:70) _____

_____

_____

Peter's Denial and Love

3. Where was Peter the second time when another maid asked him about Jesus? (Matt. 26:71) _____

4. How did Peter respond the third time when someone asked him about Jesus? (Matt. 26:73-74) _____
_____

5. What was Peter doing while he was in the palace? (Mark 14:66-67) _____
_____

6. What type of speech did Peter have? (Mark 14:70) _____

7. What were Christ's words concerning Peter's denial? (Mark 14:72) _____
_____
_____

8. Where did they take Jesus? (Luke 22:54) _____

9. When the cock crowed, what was Peter's response? (Luke 22:62) _____
_____

10. What did Christ tell Peter to do? (John 21:15) _____

Thought Questions:

1. How have you failed recently? _____
_____
_____
_____

2. What are some valuable lessons that you have learned through your failures?
_____
_____
_____
_____

Lesson Review:

1. Who is the Comforter? (Lesson#54) _____

2. Explain why Christ was not a liar. (Lesson #52) _____
_____
_____
_____

3. Why did Christ wash the disciples' feet? (Lesson #48) _____
_____

Famous Last Words
Lesson #56

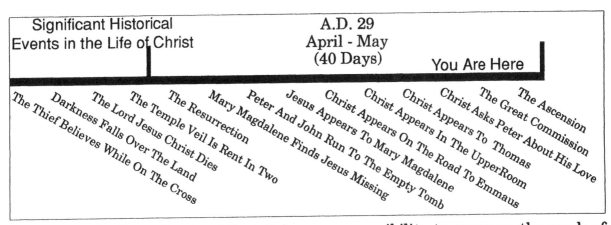

Significant Historical
Events in the Life of Christ

A.D. 29
April - May
(40 Days)

You Are Here

The Thief Believes While On The Cross
The Darkness Falls Over The Land
The Lord Jesus Christ Dies
The Temple Veil Is Rent In Two
The Resurrection
Mary Magdalene Finds Jesus Missing
Peter And John Run To The Empty Tomb
Jesus Appears To Mary Magdalene
Christ Appears On The Road To Emmaus
Christ Appears In The Upper Room
Christ Appears To Thomas
Christ Asks Peter About His Love
The Great Commission
The Ascension

<u>Lesson Goal</u>: To understand that it is our responsibility to carry on the work of Christ's kingdom.

<u>Background Text</u>: Matthew 28:16-20; Luke 24:44-53; John 21:25

<u>Memory Verse</u>: And He said unto them, Go ye into all the world, and preach the gospel to every creature. Mark 16:15

Since this is the last lesson in this study, I felt that it was important to review a significant aspect of Christ's message. As believers, it is our responsibility to carry on the work of God's kingdom. The commission that our Lord gave His disciples is the same for us. We are to go into the world to make disciples and teach them the principles of God's Word.

There are many Christians today who feel overwhelmed by the sin and corruption that is in the world. They throw their hands into the air and sigh, "What can I possibly do about it?" These believers have focused their attention upon the sin and have lost sight of their Savior. Instead of going out and trying to make a

difference in their work place, with their neighbors, where they live and where they shop, they lock themselves in their homes, hiding within their little sheltered world.

This is not the lifestyle that our Lord commanded! There is the need for Christians today who not only love the Lord and study His Word, but who also tell their neighbors about Christ, stand against the wicked teachings of

Famous Last Words

humanism, fight against sins like abortion and pornography, and raise their families with Christ at the center of their homes. The implication of the Great Commission is to permeate every area of our lives with the message and teaching of the gospel.

"But," someone will say, "I am only one voice. What effect could I possibly have in the world?" Our effect is not measured in size or quantity, but in quality. As believers, our Lord has given us the indwelling power of the Holy Spirit. There is nothing insignificant about our service for the Lord. We each have a specific calling and direction that God has given us. Whether male or female, young or old, God's message should go out to all with whom we come in contact. Whatever our sphere of influence may be, that is where we put the gospel into action. Whether at work, church, school or play, we are around people in all types of activities. Our message and ministry begin with them.

Questions: Please indicate your answer with either True or False.

1. _____ The only power that Jesus has is in heaven. (Matt. 28:18)

2. _____ We are to go and teach all nations, baptizing them in the name of the Father, Son and Holy Ghost. (Matt. 28:19)

3. _____ We are to teach them to observe all things that Jesus has commanded. (Matt. 28:20)

4. _____ Jesus is with us always, even to the end of the world. (Matt. 28:20)

5. _____ All things must be fulfilled which were written in the law of Moses, the prophets, and in the Psalms. (Luke 24:44)

6. _____ Jesus opened their understanding so they could comprehend the scriptures. (Luke 24:45)

7. _____ Repentance as remission of sins should be preached in His name. (Luke 24:47)

8. _____ We should preach His name to all nations, beginning at Jerusalem. (Luke 24:47)

9. _____ There were many other miracles Jesus did that were not recorded. (John 21:25)

10. _____ If every miracle were written down, the world could contain the books that would be written. (John 21:25)

Thought Questions:

1. What can you do to make a difference for Christ's kingdom? _____

_____

_____

_____

_____

2. Who is someone you know that has made a positive effect in society with the Gospel? What lessons can you learn from them in order to be a better Christian? _____

_____

_____

_____

_____

Lesson Review:

1. What are the four steps in coping with failure? (Lesson #55) _____

_____

_____

_____

2. Why did the two men not recognize Christ? (Lesson #54) _____

_____

3. What problems arise if you believe that the disciples made up the story of the resurrection of Christ Jesus? (Lesson #52) _____

_____

_____

_____

_____

Let dogs delight to bark and bite,　　*But, children, you should never let*
For God hath made them so;　　*Such angry passions rise;*
Let bears and lions growl and fight,　　*Your little hands were never made*
For 'tis their nature too.　　*To tear each other's eyes.*

-- Isaac Watts, Against Quarreling and Fighting

Unit Test #4

1. _____ In whose house was Jesus while He was in Bethany? (Matt. 26:6)

2. _____ Besides coming to see Jesus, who else did the people come to see? (John 12:9)

3. _____ Where were the disciples to find a colt? (Matt. 21:2)

4. _____ In whom were the disciples to have faith? (Mark 11:22)

5. _____ How much money did the poor widow give? (Mark 12:42)

6. _____ Who caused Judas to want to betray Christ? (Luke 22:3)

7. _____ Who sought opportunity to betray Christ? (Matt. 26:14-16)

8. _____ What did Jesus and the disciples do before they went to the Mount of Olives? (Mark 14:26)

9. _____ The disciples were to pray so as not to enter into what? (Luke 22:40)

10._____ How many times did Christ find his disciples sleeping? (Mark 14:41)

11._____ To whom did the chief priests and elders take Jesus? (Matt. 27:2)

12._____ On what day of the week had Jesus risen? (Mark 16:9)

13._____ Of what did the women have a vision? (Luke 24:23)

14._____ Who came to Peter when he was in the palace? (Matt. 26:69)

15._____ When is Christ with us? (Matt. 28:20)

a. Satan
b. Simon the Leper
c. The village
d. Three
e. Judas
f. A damsel
g. Angels
h. God
i. Lazarus
j. First
k. Two mites
l. Pontius Pilate
m. Temptation
n. Sang a hymn
o. Always

Definitions

Absolutes: Unchanging standards or laws which one uses to govern his life.

Altar: A structure where sacrifices are made and burned.

Anarchy: A society without laws or government.

Archaeology: The scientific study of an old culture in order to learn about the people and their lifestyle.

Attitude: Inward feelings that affect the way we act and think.

Baal: A god of nature that was worshipped by the people who lived in Canaan.

Beguile: To mislead or deceive.

Blameless: Free from guilt or wrong doing; innocent.

Bondage: The state of being subjected to external control.

Caution: Alertness or prudence in a dangerous situation.

Cherubim: Celestial beings distinguished by knowledge.

Chronological: Arranged in the order of time; from first to last.

Commitment: Given over to something or someone to insure all their needs are met.

Compromise: To lower or readjust one's standards.

Condemnation: To declare judgment and sentence for punishment.

Conduct: Personal behavior; a way of acting.

Conscience: An internal recognition of what is right or wrong.

Consequences: The results of one's own actions.

Contentment: To be pleased or satisfied in one's circumstances.

Covenant: A promise or agreement.

Covetousness: To desire wrongly without regard to the rights of others.

Cubit: A measurement used during Bible times; equal to eighteen inches in length.

Deceiver: A person who misleads another by false statement or action.

Determination: An act by which one purposes to accomplish a task.

Enmity: A feeling of hostility or hatred.

Environment: One's surroundings, conditions or influences.

Envy: A feeling of resentment or desire to possess something someone else possesses or has achieved.

Evolution: The belief that the universe developed by chance, and was not created by God in a literal six days.

Fear: A distressing emotion aroused by impending pain, danger, evil, etc.

Figurative: Not literal; representing a figure of speech.

Fool: A person who lacks common sense; a weak minded or gullible person.

Forfeit: Something to which the right is lost; give up.

Forgiveness: To grant full pardon to someone for their wrong actions.

Genealogy: An account of human ancestry from one generation to the next.

Gentile: Any nationality or race of people that is not Jewish.

Gospel: The message of salvation through belief in Jesus Christ.

Gratefulness: Warmly or deeply appreciative of kindness or benefits received.

Gullible: Easily deceived or cheated.

Holy: Godly in character; devoted to a pure life; obeying and serving God.

Humanist: A person who believes he can come to God on the basis of his own efforts and merits.

Idol: An image representing a false god.

Illustration: A picture or story used to communicate an idea.

Definitions

Inheritance: Receiving a gift or blessing as a result of one's own position or relationship to another.

Jews (Jewish): The nation or tribe of people that has as its father, Abraham. Also referred to as Hebrews and Israelites.

Justice: The moral principle of being righteous and obeying God's law.

Lapse: A failure or slight error.

Laver: A bowl or basin containing water in which to wash.

Literal: True to the fact; not exaggerated; not figurative.

Love: A strong commitment to another person or object; affection or compassion.

Messiah: The expected savior of the Jewish people; Jesus Christ.

Omer: A Hebrew unit of measurement equaling about two pints.

Oppress: To burden with cruel or unjust authority or restraints.

Pantheistic: The belief that God and nature are one; to worship nature is to worship God.

Perspective: A particular point of view.

Principle: A primary truth upon which one governs or rules his life.

Procrastination: To put off something until another day or time.

Prosperity: To have good success.

Providence: The foreseeing care and guardianship of God over His creation.

Redemption: To buy back or purchase something that belonged to someone else; deliver; rescue.

Reincarnation: The belief that the soul, upon death of the body, moves to another body or form and does not go to heaven or hell.

Repentance: Regret or sorrow for a past sin which results in a change of action.

Resisting: To withstand, strive against, or oppose.

Responsibility: Answering or accounting for something or someone under one's own power and authority.

Restitution: Restoring something that was lost, damaged or injured, either by payment or sacrifice.

Righteous: Morally pure and just; holy; obedient to God's laws.

Sacrifice: The offering of life (animal, plant, human) or some possession to a deity; to surrender or devote oneself to a Godly calling.

Salvation: Deliverance from the power and penalty of sin; redemption.

Selfless: Greater care and concern for someone or something than for oneself.

Severe: Harsh; extreme; serious.

Shewbread: The bread placed every Sabbath before Jehovah on the table beside the altar of incense, and eaten at the end of the week by the priests.

Sin: Transgression or disobedience to God's Law.

Society: A body of human beings generally associated together as a community.

Sovereign: The supreme or independent power or authority.

Spiritual: Pertaining to sacred things; Godly.

Submission: To surrender or obey; to humbly give oneself over to another.

Tabernacle: A tent used by the Israelites as a portable sanctuary before the building of the temple in Jerusalem.

Temptation: Prompting to do something that one should not do; an enticement to sin.

Theologians: Individuals who study and teach other people about God.

Tithe: The giving of one-tenth of one's income either in the form of money, produce or agriculture to the Lord and His work.

Virtue: Moral excellence or goodness.

Vocation: An occupation, profession or business; a trade or calling.

Vow: A solemn promise or pledge.

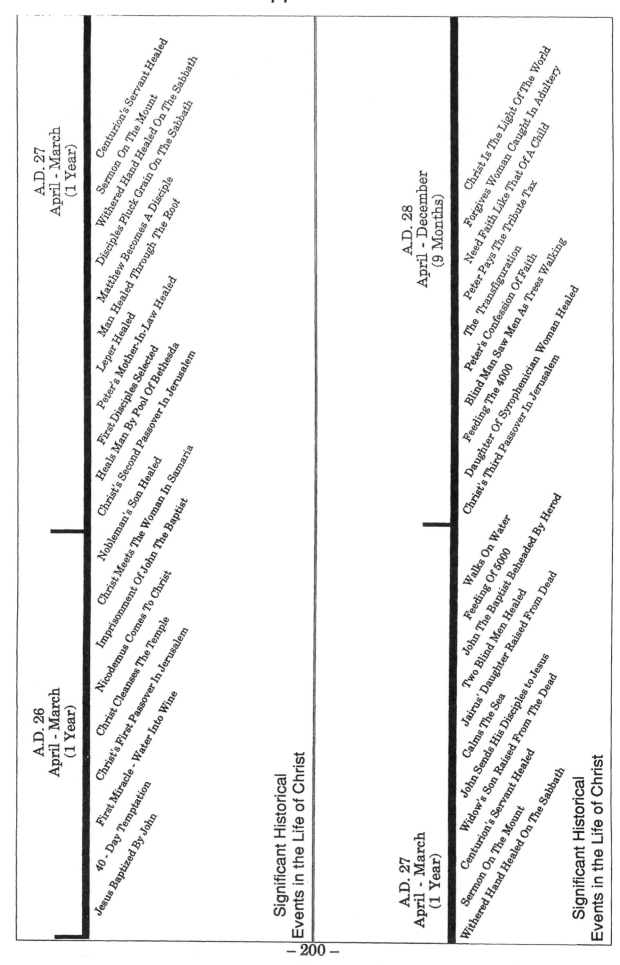

A.D. 26
April - March
(1 Year)

- Jesus Baptized By John
- 40 - Day Temptation
- First Miracle - Water Into Wine
- Christ's First Passover In Jerusalem
- Christ Cleanses The Temple
- Nicodemus Comes To Christ
- Imprisonment Of John The Baptist
- Christ Meets The Woman In Samaria
- Nobleman's Son Healed

A.D. 27
April - March
(1 Year)

- Christ's Second Passover In Jerusalem
- Heals Man By Pool Of Bethesda
- First Disciples Selected
- Peter's Mother-In-Law Healed
- Leper Healed
- Man Healed Through The Roof
- Matthew Becomes A Disciple
- Disciples Pluck Grain On The Sabbath
- Withered Hand Healed On The Sabbath
- Sermon On The Mount
- Centurion's Servant Healed

Significant Historical
Events in the Life of Christ

A.D. 27
April - March
(1 Year)

- Withered Hand Healed On The Sabbath
- Sermon On The Mount
- Centurion's Servant Healed
- Widow's Son Raised From The Dead
- John Sends His Disciples to Jesus
- Jairus' Daughter Raised From Dead
- Calms The Sea
- Two Blind Men Healed
- John The Baptist Beheaded By Herod
- Feeding Of 5000
- Walks On Water

A.D. 28
April - December
(9 Months)

- Christ's Third Passover In Jerusalem
- Daughter Of Syrophenician Woman Healed
- Feeding The 4000
- Blind Man Saw Men As Trees Walking
- Peter's Confession Of Faith
- The Transfiguration
- Peter Pays The Tribute Tax
- Need Faith Like That Of A Child
- Forgives Woman Caught In Adultery
- Christ Is The Light Of The World

Significant Historical
Events in the Life of Christ

Studying God's Word Book G

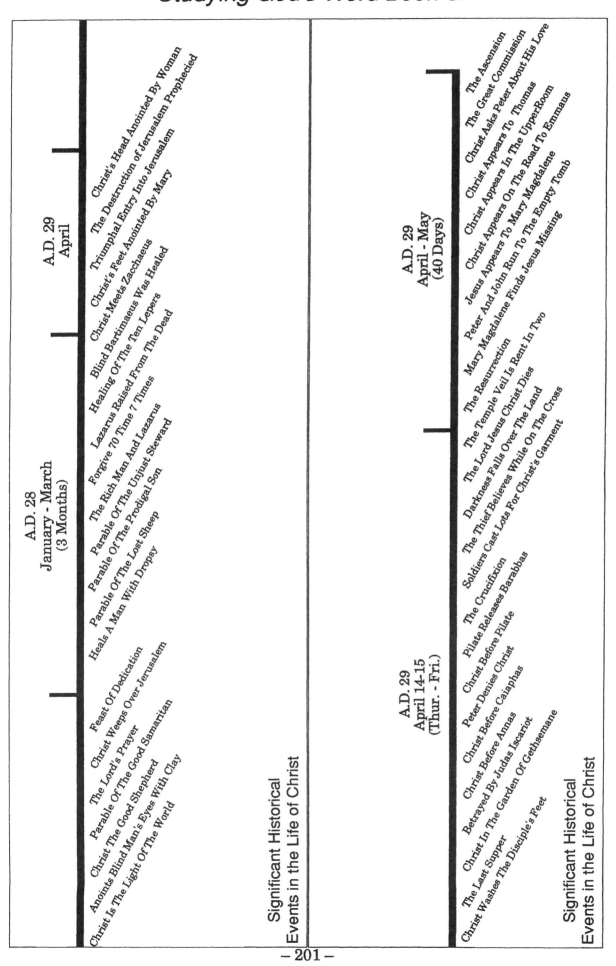

Significant Historical
Events in the Life of Christ

Significant Historical
Events in the Life of Christ

Appendix B

A =   N =

B =   O =

C =   P =

D =   Q =

E =   R =

F =   S =

G =   T =

H =   U =

I =   V =

J =   W =

K =   X =

L =   Y =

M =   Z =

Appendix C

The Greek Alphabet

Capital Letters	Small Letters	Name	Pronunciation
A	α	Alpha	a as in father (long)
			a as in bat (short)
B	β	Beta	b as in ball
Γ	γ	Gamma	g as in gift
Δ	δ	Delta	d as in debt
E	ε	Epsilon	e as in met
Z	ζ	Zeta	dz as in adz
H	η	Eta	e as in obey
Θ	θ	Theta	th as in theme
I	ι	Iota	i as in magazine (long)
			i as in pit (short)
K	κ	Kappa	k as in kin
Λ	λ	Lambda	l as in long
M	μ	Mu	m as in man
N	ν	Nu	n as in no
Ξ	ξ	Xi	x as in relax
O	o	Omicron	o as in omelet
Π	π	Pi	p as in pay
P	ρ	Rho	r as in ring
Σ	σ, ς	Sigma	s as in sing
T	τ	Tau	t as in tale
Y	υ	Upsilon	u as in unity
Φ	φ	Phi	ph as in phonetics
X	χ	Chi	ch as in chemial
Ψ	ψ	Psi	ps as in taps
Ω	ω	Omega	o as in tone

Note: The definition of a word is oftentimes determined by the context in which it is used. Just as in the English language when we say, "The girl can kick the can," the definition of the word "can" is determined by the way it is used in the sentence.

Appendix C

The Greek Dictionary

αγαπην -- love
αιωνιον -- everlasting
αληθειας (αληθεια) -- truth
αλλ -- but, except, yet
απολ
ηται -- perish
αρχη -- beginning
αυτω (αυτον, αυτου) -- him, his
δι -- by
δοξαν -- glory, radiance
ειμι -- myself
εις -- in
εγενετο -- became
εγω -- I
ει -- definite article (not always used or translated into English): the
εμου -- me
εν -- preposition with location and sphere: in, on, by, among
εθεασαμεθα -- we beheld
ερχεται -- comes, appear, go
εσκηνωσεν -- dwelt
εχει -- has, hold
εχη -- possess, preserve
γαρ -- so
η -- definite article: the
ηγαπησεν -- loved, cherished
ημιν -- us
ην -- was
ινα -- that
Ιησους-- Jesus
και -- conjunction: and, also
κοσμον -- world, order

λογος (λεγει) -- word
μειζονα -- greater
μη -- but
μη αποληται -- may not perish
μονογενη -- uniquely begotten one
μονογενους -- belonging
ο -- the
οδος -- way (road)
ουδεις -- no one
ουτως -- for
παρα -- to the, beside
πας -- all
πατρος (πατερα) -- father
πληρης -- filled with
πιστευων -- ones who believe
προς -- preposition with location: with, at, to, toward
σαρξ -- flesh
ταυτης -- than this
την -- definite article: the
τις -- one
τον -- definite article: the
των -- definite article: the
θεος (θεον) -- God
θη υπερ -- should lay down for
υιον -- son
ψυχην -- life
φιλων -- friends
χαριτος -- grace
ως -- as
ωστε -- creation
ζωη (ζωην) -- life

COMPARISONS OF THE FOUR GOSPELS

	MATTHEW	MARK	LUKE	JOHN
View of Christ:	Jewish Messiah "King"	Divine Servant	Son of Man	Son of God
Destination:	Jews	Romans	Greeks	World
Key Verse:	Matthew 5:17	Mark 10:45	Luke 19:10	20:30-31
Theme:	Christ's offer of His Kingdom to the Jews	Christ's ministry of obedience to the Father	Christ's response to men's needs	Christ's deity
Distinctives:	Fulfillment of the Old Testament prophecies	Greek "eutheos" (immediately) used forty times; shortest gospel	Completeness and detail; longest Gospel	Believe to have eternal life (forms of believe used 99 times)
Nature of Book:	Prophetical	Practical	Historical	Spiritual
Key Words:	"Fulfilled"	"Immediately"	"Son of Man"	"Believe"
Uniqueness:	58% (42% unique)	93 % (7% unique)	41% (59% unique)	8% (92% unique)
Emphasis on:	Sermons	Miracles	Parables	Doctrine
Written by:	Tax collector	Servant or missionary	Physician	Fisherman
Prophetic Aspect:	King (Zech. 9:9)	Servant (Is. 41:1)	Man (Zech. 6:12)	God (Is. 40:9)
Work of Christ:	Christ in His sovereignty come to reign and rule	Christ in His humility come to serve and suffer	Christ in His humanity come to share and sympathize	Christ in His deity come to reveal and redeem
Time Viewpoint:	Past	Present	Future	Eternal
Genealogy:	To Abraham		To Adam	

References

Barnes, Albert, <u>Barnes Notes</u>,
Grand Rapids, MI: Baker Book House, 1949.

Beers, V. Gilbert, <u>The Victor Handbook of Bible Knowledge</u>,
Wheaton, IL: Victory Books, 1981.

Bryant, T. Alton, ed., <u>The New Compact Bible Dictionary</u>,
Grand Rapids, MI: Zondervan Publishing House, 1967.

Calvin, John, <u>Calvin's Commentaries</u>,
Grand Rapids, MI: Baker Book House.

Davis, J.D., <u>Illustrated Davis Dictionary of the Bible</u>,
Nashville, TN: Royal Publishers, 1973.

De Graaf, S.G., <u>Promise and Deliverance</u>, Four Volumes,
St. Catharines, Ontario, Canada: Paideia Press, 1977.

<u>Encyclopedia Britannica</u>, 1898 edition,
The Werner Company, 1898.

Frank, Harry Thomas, ed., <u>Hammond Atlas of the Bible Lands</u>,
Maplewood, NJ: Hammond Inc., 1977.

Gromacki, Robert G., <u>New Testament Survey</u>,
Grand Rapids, MI: Baker Book House, 1974.

Hall, Terry, <u>Bible Panorama</u>,
Wheaton, IL: Victory Books, 1983.

Halley, H.H., <u>Halley Bible Handbook</u>,
Chicago, IL: Halley, 1927.

Harrison, Everett F. & Pfeiffer, Charles F., ed., <u>The Wycliffe Bible Commentary</u>,
Chicago, IL: Moody Press, 1976.

Hovey, Bill, <u>New Testament Time Line</u>,
Time Line Resource, 1974.

<u>International Standard Bible Encyclopedia</u>,
Grand Rapids, MI: Eerdmans Publishing Co., 1939.

Klassen, Frank R., <u>The Chronology of the Bible</u>,
Nashville, TN: Regal Publishing Co. Inc., 1975.

Morris, William, ed., <u>The American Heritage Dictionary of the English Language</u>,
Boston, MA: Houghton Mifflin Company, 1980.

<u>New Bible Dictionary</u>,
Wheaton, IL: Tyndale House Publishers, Inc., 1962.

<u>Pocket Book of Quotations</u>,
New York, NY: Pocket Books, 1942.

Ryle, J.C., <u>Ryles Expository Thoughts on the Gospels</u>,
Grand Rapids, MI: Baker Book House, Reprinted 1977.

Ryrie, Charles, <u>The Ryrie Study Bible</u>,
Chicago, IL: Moody Press, 1976.

Scofield, C.I., <u>New Scofield Reference Bible</u>,
New York, NY: Oxford University Press, 1967.

Strong, James, <u>Strong's Concordance</u>,
Riverside Book and Bible, Iowa Falls, IA.

Summers, Ray, <u>Essentials of New Testament Greek</u>,
Nashville, TN: Broadman Press, 1950.

Tenney, Merrill C., <u>John: The Gospel of Belief</u>,
Grand Rapids, MI: Eerdmans Publishing Co., 1948.

Thayer, Joseph H., <u>Thayers Greek-English Lexicon of the New Testament</u>,
Grand Rapids, MI: Baker Book House, 1977.

Vine, W.E., <u>Vine's Expository Dictionary</u>,
Old Tappan, NJ: Fleming H. Revell, 1981.

List of Illustrations

Notes